THE AMERICAN

HOME COOK BOOK,

WITH

Several Hundred Excellent Recipes,

SELECTED AND TRIED WITH GREAT CARE, AND WITH A VIEW TO BE USED
BY THOSE WHO REGARD ECONOMY, AND CONTAINING IMPOR-
TANT INFORMATION ON THE ARRANGEMENT AND
WELL ORDERING OF THE KITCHEN.

THE WHOLE BASED ON MANY YEARS OF EXPERIENCE.

BY AN AMERICAN LADY.

ILLUSTRATED WITH ENGRAVINGS.

PRYOR PUBLICATIONS
WHITSTABLE AND WALSALL

PRYOR PUBLICATIONS
WHITSTABLE AND WALSALL

Specialist in Facsimile Reproductions.

MEMBER OF
INDEPENDENT PUBLISHERS GUILD

75 Dargate Road, Yorkletts, Whitstable,
Kent CT5 3AE, England.
Tel. & Fax: (01227) 274655

Email: alan@pryor-publish.clara.net

http://home.clara.net/pryor-publish

Kent Exporter of the Year Awards Winner 1998

© Pryor Publications 1999

May 2000

ISBN 0 946014 85 X

A full list of Titles sent free on request

First published in 1854
by Dick and Fitzgerald
of New York, price 30c

Printed by
Hillman Printers
(Frome) Ltd
Handlemaker Road,
Marston Trading Estate,
Frome, Somerset BA11 4RW.
Tel: 01373 473526   Fax: 01373 451852

PREFACE

THE present work has been designed and written entirely with a view to *practical utility*, and for the information of those young Housekeepers who have not had the benefit of regular instructions in the affairs of the kitchen. My reason for attempting to compose such a work, may be explained in a few words. All the cookery books, both of an old and new date, which I have been able to procure, appear to be written chiefly as remembrancers for professed cooks, or as guides in the extensive kitchen of the wealthy, where economy is not supposed to be a matter of importance. The greater part of their recipes are consequently written on a principle of lavish expenditure, and refer to a great number of things that are never seen at the tables of the frugal and industrious. Excellent, therefore, as many of these works are, they are generally unsuitable for popular and practical use ; young or unexperienced persons who have occasion to consult them upon emergencies, uniformly complain *that they cannot understand them*, and that, if they did, they could not *afford* to follow them as guides. It is with the humble hope of (at least in some measure) remedying these deficiencies that the present work is presented to the public. It has, I have said, been designed expressly for the use of housekeepers who study simplicity and economy in the preparation of food, and who require explicit directions for their guidance. *Every recipe,— every advice—every little piece of information, is the result of personal experience.* I have set down nothing on trust, or merely because others have said it; and in all parts have endeavored to write in so plain a manner—detailing one by one every step in the process of preparing the various dishes—that any inexperienced person, I should think, could find no difficulty both in comprehending the directions and acting upon them.

It would have been very easy to extend the work to double or treble its present size, by adding a mass of miscellaneous recipes usually appended to works professing to inculcate domestic economy. But I judged it to be preferable to present an *useful* and *cheap* rather than a bulky work; and as it is, I believe that nothing of the least consequence has been omitted

It may not however be out of place *here* to announce that the authoress has in preparation a "Home Receipt Book" which she designs to be a complete manual for all that relates to House cleaning—Dying—Repairing—Home made beverages—accidents—emergencies—the sick room—remedies—and all the thousand and one things that the head of a family requires to know.

INTRODUCTORY REMARKS.

COOKERY is an art upon which so much of our daily comfort and health depends, that it is of the highest importance that it be well performed. Every housewife may not be able to procure the finest kinds of food, but every one has it in her power to make the most of that which she does procure.

By a certain degree of skill and attention, very humble fare may be dressed in such a manner that it will almost rival the most expensive dishes, in both savouriness and nutritiousness A good housewife suffers nothing to be lost or spoiled. Mere scraps which a careless individual would perhaps throw away, are put to a proper use, and, by means of certain auxiliary seasoning, brought to table in a new and attractive guise. Even if little or nothing be absolutely saved by these economical arrangements, the dressing of food in a tasteful manner is a point of some importance. When a dish has a slovenly appearance, is smoked, underdone, or prepared with rancid or unclean seasoning, both the eye and the appetite are offended, which is a serious evil in itself, independently of the injury which may possibly be done to the stomach of the eater. In every respect therefore, it is consistent with good judgment to prepare food for the table in the most tasteful and agreeable

Another essential point in cookery is *attention*. Many persons think they have done all that is necessary, when they have fairly commenced or set a-going any particular process in cooking, they seem to imagine that they may safely leave a roast to roast by itself, or leave a pot with broth to boil by itself, and that they have only to go back to the fire at a certain time, and that they will find the thing ready for dishing. Now, this kind of inattention is certain to spoil the best meat ever put to fire.

Some processes require much less attention than others, but none can be properly performed if left long to itself.

A good cook is pretty frequent in her visits to the fire to see how the operation of dressing is going on, and seize the proper moment in giving her assistance.

A kitchen should always be well furnished; there is no necessity that it should be profusely so, but there should be a sufficiency of every thing which can aid in producing the dishes preparing, with the success which is so essential to the gratification of the palate. A good workman cannot work well with bad tools, neither can good cooks do justice to their proficiency if they possess not the necessary utensils suitable to the various modes of cooking. And when this important point has been realized, *cleanliness in every article used* should *be scrupulously observed;* no utensil should be suffered to be put away dirty, it not only injures the article itself materially, to say nothing of the impropriety of the habit, but prevents its readiness for use on any sudden occasion. No *good* cook or servant would be guilty of such an act; those who are, do so either from laziness or want of system, or a nature naturally dirty; if a very strong hint will not suffice, it is of little use speaking out, for it would be the result of a bad habit, that no talking in the world would cure. A servant who is inherently dirty or slovenly, should never be retained, it is better and easier to change frequently until the mistress is suited, however unpleasant frequent changes may prove, than Quixotically attempt to cure a person of this description. Cleanliness is the most essential ingredient in the art of cooking, and at any personal sacrifice should be maintained in the kitchen.

In furnishing a kitchen there should be everything likely to be required, but not one article more than is wanted; unnecessary profusion creates a litter; a deficiency too often sacrifices the perfection of a dish, there should be a sufficiency and no more.

The following articles, of which we have given engravings, are requisite, and may be procured at any first-class Housekeeper's Furnishing store.

1

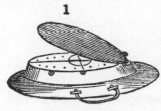

1 *Waffle Furnace.*—A very ingenious article, making four good-sized waffles with less labor than is required in making one with the ordinary iron.

Waffle Furnace.

2

2 *Chafing Dish* with alcohol lamp, to keep steaks hot, or to cook oysters, venison, mutton, &c., on the table.

3

3 *Lignumvitae Mortar and Pestle.*—The adulteration of ground spices, makes this an important article where *good* spices are wanted.

4 *Whip Churn.*—For making whip cream syllabub, &c.

5 *Knife-cleaning Machine.*—By the use of which knives need never be put in water, and are kept bright with less time or trouble than in the old fashioned way.

6 *Water Filter*—For purifying cistern water for cooking or table use.

7 *Wire Dish Covers.*—To cover meats, pastry, milk, butter, &c., from dust, flies &c., in the pantry or on the table.

Wire Dish Covers,

8 *Ice Cream Freezer and Moulds.*

8 *Patent Ice Cream Freezer.* —By which Creams, Ices &c., can be frozen fit for table use in a very few minutes. The forms are easily managed and now coming into general family use.

9 *The Japanned Tin Boxes* keep cake, bread, &c., perfectly fresh without the undesirable moisture of the stone jar.

10 *Tea and Coffee Caddies.*

11 *The Spice Box.*—Has six separate boxes that take out, so that whole or ground spices may be kept nice and separate.

12

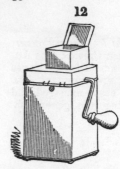

12 *French Julienne Mill.*—To cut into fin parings all kinds of vegetables for soup.

13

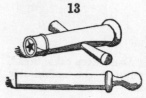

13 *French Butter Forcer.*—There are 12 different forms to each, that give an infinite variety to this decorative manner of serving butter.

14

14 *Coffee Roaster.*—To each pound of coffee put one table-spoonful of water. The coffee will thoroughly roast without being burned.

15

15 *Sauce Pan and Potato Steamer.*

16

16 *Butter Pat in Case.*—This gives the butter a handsome form and print at the same time.

17

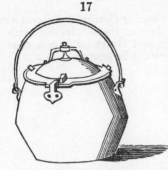

Soup Digester.

17 *Soup Digester.*—The great importance of this valuable utensil, the *Digester* not only to poor families, but to the public in general, in producing a larger quantity of wholesome and nourishing food, by a much cheaper method than has ever been hitherto obtained, is a matter of such serious and interesting consideration, as cannot be too earnestly recommended to those who make economy in the support of their families an object of their attention. The chief, and indeed the only thing necessary to be done, is to direct a proper mode of using it to most advantage; and this mode is both simple and easy. Care must be taken in filling the digester, to leave room enough for the steam to pass off through the valve at the top of the cover. This may be done by filling the digester only three parts full of water and bruised bones or meat, which it is to be noticed are all to be put in together. It must then be placed near a slow fire, so as only to simmer (more heat injures the quality,) and this it must do for the space of eight or ten hours. After this has been done, the soup is to be strained through a hair sieve or cullender, in order to separate any bits of bones. The soup is then to be put into the digester again, and after whatever vegetables, spices, &c., are thought necessary are added, the whole is to be well boiled together for an hour or two, and it will be then fit for immediate use. In putting on the lid of the digester, take care that a mark, thus (X) on the lid, is opposite to a similar one on the digester. The digester may also be obtained to contain from four quarts to ten gallons. There are also saucepan and stewpan digesters to hold from one to eight quarts.

18

18 *Roasting Screen and Jack.*—The screen is adapted to the ranges and cooking stoves in general use. The jack is wound up and runs so as to keep the meat constantly turning till cooked.

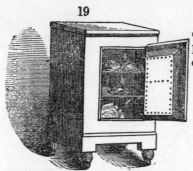

19 *Closet or Upright Refrigerator.* The door on the side insures ventilation, and the closet form is most convenient to arrange dishes.

20 *Fish Scissors.*—For cutting and trimming fish.

21 *French Bake Pan.*—Of wrought iron, to put fire or embers on the cover if needful.

22 *Patent Ice Breaker.*— To break ice for table use, and for making ice cream.

23 *Cheese Toaster.*—To make Welsh Rarebit, with double bottom for hot water.

24 *Charlotte Russ Pans.*—Oval shape, and nice to bake any other kind of cake.

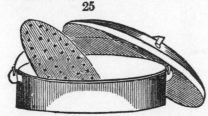

25 *Fish Kettle.*—With strainer, to boil fish and take it out whole.

Fish Kettles, various sizes.

26 *French Basting Spoons.*—Deep and with side handles.

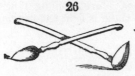

27 *Russia Iron Roll, or Corn Cake Pan.*—Gives a handsome brown soft under-crust.

28 *Enamelled Preserving Pan.*—For sweet meats, jellies. marmalade, &c.

29 *French Milk Sauce Pans.*—To boil milk, cook custards, &c., without boiling over, by an arrangement of valves in the lid.

30

30 *Copper Cake Form.*—To bake cake for icing.

31

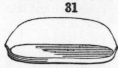

31 *Soap Stone Griddle* —To bake cakes with out grease or smell.

32

32 *Marble Slab, and Marble Rolling Pin.* —Pastry made with these is light and flaky, from its being cold.

33   34

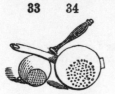

33 *Gravy Strainer.*

34 *Soup Strainer.*

35

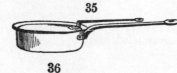

Copper Stew Pan.—Tinned inside.

36

36 *Egg Coddler.*—To cook eggs on the breakfast table.

37

37 *Wine Cooler.*—For cooling bottles of wine, &c.

38

38 *Jelly Strainer.*—Is made double and filled in with hot water, this heat keeps the mass limpid and a much greater amount of jelly is made from the same materials.

39   40

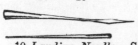

39 *Ala Mode Needle.*—With split end to draw in strips of fat pork, bacon, &c., into beef for a-la-moding.

40 *Larding Needle.*—Same for poultry, game, &c.

41

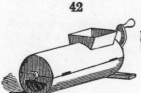

Flesh Fork.—To take ham, boiled meat, &c. from the pot.

42

(see illustration below)

42 *Sausage Meat Cutter.*—Will cut four pounds of meat per minute for sausages, hash, &c

43

Iron handle. steel blade *Chop Knife.*

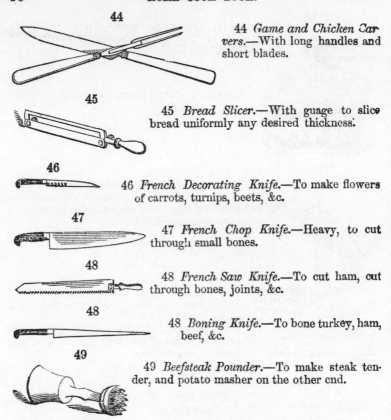

44 *Game and Chicken Carvers.*—With long handles and short blades.

45 *Bread Slicer.*—With guage to slice bread uniformly any desired thickness.

46 *French Decorating Knife.*—To make flowers of carrots, turnips, beets, &c.

47 *French Chop Knife.*—Heavy, to cut through small bones.

48 *French Saw Knife.*—To cut ham, cut through bones, joints, &c.

48 *Boning Knife.*—To bone turkey, ham, beef, &c.

49 *Beefsteak Pounder.*—To make steak tender, and potato masher on the other end.

50 *Beefsteak Tongs.*—To turn a steak, to avoid puncturing holes with a fork, which lets the juice escape.

51

Oval Pot.—For boiling ham, corned beef &c

52

Porcelain Lemon Squeezer.—To preserve the fine oil of the lemon that is usually absorbed by the wooden squeezer.

53

53 *Fancy Patty Pans.*—For baking ornamental tea cakes.

54

54 *Oval Omelet Pan.*

55

55 *Boxwood Scrub-brush.*—To clean beautifully unpainted wood, table tops. meat and pastry boards.

56

56 *Fry Pan.*

57

57 *Vegetable Slicer.*—To slice potatoes, to fry and fricasee, green corn from the cob, cucumbers vegetables for soup, cabbage, dried beef, &c.

58

58 *Felt Jelly Bag.*—Is seamless and strains jelly handsomely.

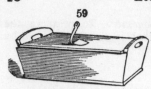

59 *Wooden Bread Trough and Scraper*
For mixing bread.

60 Revolving Enamelled Gridiron with
fluted bars to convey the gravy to the cup.

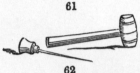

61 Ice mallet with pick that slides into
the handle.

62 Wire corn popper, a half tea cup full of
dry pop corn will fill the popper by being agit
ated over the fire.

63 Water cooler, filled in with charcoal, preserves
the ice and keeps water icy cold.—The water is
kept cooler than the atmosphere without ice.

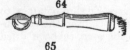

64 Sardine opener, to open tin boxes of sar-
dines, preserved meats, preserves &c.

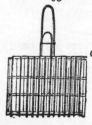

65 Double wire oyster gridiron to broil oysters, chops
cutlets, steaks, toast bread &c.

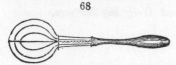

66 Wire pea or vegetable boiler, for peas, beans, rice, boils dry and when taken out no grains are left in the pot.

67 *Tea Boiler.*—The leaves are put into the ball and then the ball into the tea pot, the tea steeps without having the leaves poured into the cup.

68 *Flat egg-whip.*—The best shape and easily cleaned.

Egg Whip, various patterns,

69 *Pudding Mould.*—Who likes boiled pudding? can have it dry and light if cooked in one of these moulds.

70 *French Oval Meat Pie Mould.*—Opens at one end.

71 *Pastry Cutter.*—Various patterns

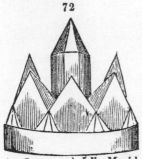

72 *Jelly or Blanc Mange Mould.*

Ice Cream and Jelly Mould

73 *Plated Fish Carver and Fork.*--Usefu also to serve asparagus, buckwheat cakes. &c

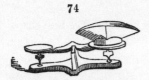

74 *Improved Weighing Balance.*

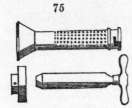

75 *Puree Presser.*—For pressing vegetables for soups, pulping fish, &c.

76 *Egg Poacher.*—Break an egg in each cup and sub merse the whole in hot water.

Egg Poacher.

77 *French Sugar Scoop.*

78 *Farina Boiler Double.*—Place water in the outer boiler and cook the farina, custard, corn starch milk, &c., in the inner one.

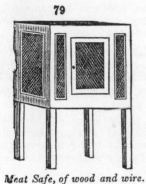

79 *Meat Safe.*—To protect food from mice, insects, &c.

Meat Safe, of wood and wire.

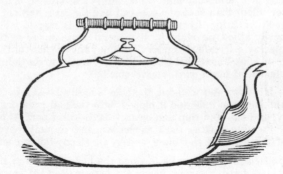

MARKETING;

AND ON THE CHOICE OF VARIOUS ARTICLES OF DIET

To Choose Beef.—Good ox beef has an open grain, and yields easily to the pressure of the finger ; it is smooth and juicy, of a rich carnation· colour in the lean, and the fat is of a fine cream-colour ; rich without being oily, firm without being hard. It is small in the bone, and full in the flesh.

Mutton.—In choosing mutton select that which is of a rich red colour, close in the grain and of a silky texture, juicy and lively in appearance, and whitish in the fat, but not shiny and tallowy. The flesh should pinch tender, and rise again when dented

Lamb.—Observe the neck vein in the fore quarter, which should be of an azure-blue to denote quality and sweetness. The flesh should be light-coloured and juicy, the fat white and rich, the bones thin and small. Lamb should be dressed while perfectly fresh or the flavor will be destroyed.

Venison.—Pass a knife along the bones of the haunches and shoulders ; if it smell sweet, the meat is new and good ; if tainted, the fleshy parts of the sides will look discoloured, and the darker in proportion to its staleness. The clefts of the hoofs of young venison are close and smooth.

Veal.—The lean of good, well-fed veal, is white, smooth, and juicy ; the fat is white, firm, and abundant. The flesh of a bull-calf is firmer and of a deeper colour than that of a cow-calf, and the fat is harder ; they are equally good for eating, if young and well fed. It is easy to tell whether veal be newly killed, or stale, by its general appearance, as the colour changes quickly, particularly under the kidney and the flaps of the breast The flesh of stale-killed veal feels moist and clammy, the joints flabby and pliable, and it has a faint, musty smell.

Pork.—If young and well-fed, the lean is easily broken between the fingers, and the skin indented if nipped with the nail ; the fat is white and waxy, and the rind thin and clean. Stale-killed pork is easily detected by the skin looking dark on the top, and clammy between the creases of the legs and shoulders, and by its strong-tainted smell.

Ham and Bacon.—Run a knife along the bone of a ham ; if it come out clean, and have a savory flavor, the ham is good ; if smeared and dulled, it is spoiled either by taint or rust. Hocks and gammons of bacon may be proved in the same way. Good bacon is red in the lean and the fat is white, firm, and pulpy ; the rind is fine and thin. If it be sheathed with yellow, it is rusty and unfit for use.

Poultry.—In selecting poultry choose those that are full grown, but not old. When young and fresh-killed the eyes are full and bright, the joints neither stiff nor flabby; the skin thin and tender, so that it may be easily torn with a pin; the breast-bone is pliable, yielding easily to pressure. Fowls, if young, have a hard close vent, and the legs and comb are smooth. A goose, if young, has but few hairs, a yellow bill and is limber-footed. Ducks, when fat, are hard and thick on the belly, if young and good they are limber-footed.

Eggs.—Put your tongue to the larger end; if it feel warm, the egg is fresh; or put the egg into a pan of cold water; if perfectly fresh it will sink immediately, and so in proportion to its freshness; a rotten egg will float on the top of the water.

Butter.—The only way to try butter is by the smell and taste; never trust to its external appearance. Do not buy that which is speckled with pinky spots, nor that which has a milky appearance; such butter has not been well washed from the butter-milk, and will quickly turn sour or lose its flavor.

Fish.—The best are thick and firm. When fresh they have stiff fins, bright scales, red gills, and eyes full and bright. Freshness is best indicated by the smell. In proportion to the time they have been out of the water are they soft and flabby, the fins pliable, the scales dim, the gills dark, and the eyes sunken. Cod should be firm, white, clear, and transparent. Salmon, mackerel, herrings, &c., are chosen by their brightness and brilliancy of colour. Shell-fish, such as lobsters, and crabs, can only be chosen by the smell, and by opening them at the joint to discover whether or not they are well filled, for they sometimes feel heavy through being charged with water. If a lobster be fresh, the tail will be stiff, and spring back sharply if pulled up. A *cock* lobster may be known by the narrowness of the back part of his tail and the stiffness of the two uppermost fins within it, while those of the *hen* are soft, and the back of her tail is broader

---

IMPORTANT HINTS TO COOKS,

Which they will not regret following with attention.

Let there be a place for every article, and when not in use let every article be in its place.

Keep every utensil clean and ready for immediate use.

Keep your meat in a cool dry place, your fish on ice, and your vegetables on a stone floor free from air.

Cut your soap when it comes in, and let it dry slowly.

Keep your sweet herbs in paper bags, each bag containing only one description of herb. They should be dried in the wind and not in the sun, and when ordered in a receipt should be cautiously used, as a preponderance in any seasoning spoils it.

When oranges or lemons are used for juice, chop down the peel, put them in small pots and tie them down for use.

Apples.—In choosing apples, be guided by the weight; the heaviest are the best, and those should always be selected which, on being pressed by the thumb, yield with a slight crackling noise. Prefer large apples to small, for waste is saved in peeling and coring.

Apples should be kept on dry straw in a dry place, and pears hung up by the stalk.

Batter for fish, meat, fritters, &c.—Prepare it with fine flour, salt, a little oil, beer, vinegar, or white wine, and the whites of eggs beaten up; when of a proper thickness, about the size of a nutmeg, it will drop out of the spoon at once. Fry in oil or hog's lard.

Carrots, if young, need only be wiped when boiled—if old they must be scraped before boiling. Slice them into a dish, and pour over them melted butter.

Cauliflowers.—Cut off the stalks, but leave a little of the green on boil in spring water with a little salt in it: they must not boil too fast.

Celery.—Very little is sufficient for soups, as the flavor is very predominating. It should be particularly cleanly washed and curled when sent to table. To curl celery, wash well, and take off the outside stalks, cut it to a proper length, split each stalk into three or four divisions with a large needle, then place the head of celery in spring water with the root uppermost, and let it remain for four or five hours —it may then be tastefully arranged on the dish.

Game may often be made fit for eating when it seems spoiled, by cleaning it and washing with vinegar and water. Birds that are not likely to keep, should be drawn, cropped, and picked, then wash in two or three waters, and rub them with salt; have in readiness a large saucepan of boiling water, and plunge them into it one by one, drawing them up and down by the legs, so that the water may pass through them. Let them stay for five or six minutes, then hang them up in a cold place; when they are completely drained, well salt and pepper the insides, and thoroughly wash them before roasting.

Suet, may be kept a year, thus: choose the firmest and most free from skin or veins, remove all traces of these, put the suet in a saucepan at some distance from the fire, and let it melt gradually; when melted, pour it into a pan of cold spring water; when hard, wipe it dry, fold it in white paper, put in a linen bag, and keep it in a cool dry place; when used, it must be scraped, and will make an excellent crust with or without butter.

Tongue, which has been dried, should be soaked in water three or four hours, one which has not been dried will require little soaking; put it in cold water, and boil gently till tender.

In furnishing utensils for cooking, it is advisable to purchase *iron* saucepans; although they are more expensive at first, with care they will last a lifetime. The lids should fit close but easy.

All saucepans, dish-covers, and spoons, with the dripping-pan and ladle, should be washed in hot water immediately they are done with, they should then be turned down to drain, and afterwards wiped perfectly dry. The lids should be carefully washed, as the dirt lodges in the crevices, which, if not removed every day, will soon form a hard crust of black grease very difficult to remove.

The best thing to clean bright tin with is oil and rottenstone. This removes all kinds of stain. They should be polished off with clean soft wash-leather.

The blades of the knives and the prongs of the forks should be dipped into hot water as soon as they are removed from the dinner-table, and then wiped dry on a clean cloth; they are thus far easier to clean. They must then be rubbed on a board with bath-brick, and the prongs of the fork must be cleaned with a bit of leather put round a stick of wood. After they are clean and bright they should be wiped free from dust, and the handles should be passed through a damp cloth, and then wiped dry.

Pudding-cloths require only to be well washed out in the water in which the pudding has been boiled, and afterwards rinsed in clean hot water, and hung up to dry. It is a good plan to have an eyelet-hole in the corner, through which the string may be passed after using; it is then always ready when wanted.

After washing the plates and dishes, which require very hot water, and after rinsing in cold, if you have not a plate-rack, turn them down to drain; if they require wiping, use a clean soft cloth for the purpose, and rub them quite bright and shining. Nothing is more offensive than to handle a plate that looks dull, and feels sticky to the hand.

When commencing to cook your dinner, you will save much time and labor by placing all the things likely to be wanted on the dresser or table; at the same time it is not well to accumulate too many articles; therefore clear as you go on. You will thus avoid confusion, and always have a clear kitchen.

The plates and dishes should be placed in a screen or on a footman before the fire as soon as the cooking begins. Hot plates are indispensable to the enjoyment of a good dinner.

The fire should be made up in good time, and the saucepans for puddings and vegetables should be set on early.

A good housewife always take care to have plenty of hot water.

Cold water cracks hot iron infallibly.

In the receipts through this book, though the quantities may be accurately directed as possible, yet much must be left to the discretion of the person who uses them.

The different tastes of people require more or less of the flavor of spices, salt, butter, &c which can never be ordered by general rules, and if the cook has not a good taste, not all the ingredients which nature and art can furnish, will give exquisite flavor to her dishes, the proper articles should be at hand, and she must proportion them until the true *zest* be obtained.

2

DIRECTIONS FOR CARVING.

As the manner in which joints, and other provisions, are carved makes a material difference in the consumption and comfort of a family, it becomes highly important to those who study economy and good order in their domestic arrangements, to practise the art. We therefore recommend them to study the rules we purpose laying down, and which we commence with directions for carving fish. Our papers upon this subject will be accompanied with excellent illustrations. It must be remembered that in carving more depends upon skill than on strength; that the carving-knife should be light, and of moderate size, with a keen edge; and that the dish should be so placed as to give the operator complete command over the joint.

Fish.

Fish is served with a fish-slice, and requires very little carving, care being required, however, not to break the flakes, which, from their size, add much to the beauty of cod and salmon. Serve part of the roe, milt, or liver, to each person. The heads of carp, part of those of cod and salmon, are likewise considered delicacies.

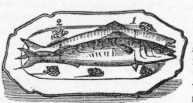

Mackerel

Should be deprived of the head and tail by passing the slice across in the direction of lines 1 and 2; they should then be divided down the back, so as to assist each person to a side; but if less is required, the thicker end should be given, as it is more esteemed. If the roe is asked for, it will be found between 1 and 2.

Cod's Head and Shoulders.

Pass the fish-slice or knife from 1 to 6 down to the bone; then help pieces from between 1—2, and 3—4, and with each slice give a piece of the sound, which lies under the back-bone, and is procured by passing the knife in the direction 4—5. There are many delicate parts about the head, particularly the oyster which is the cheek, below the eye: and a great deal of the jelly kind, which lies about the jaws. The tongue and palate are considered delicacies, and are obtained by passing the slice or a spoon into the mouth.

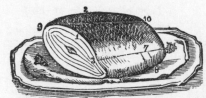

Salmon.

Give a portion of the back and belly to each person, or as desired. If a whole salmon is served remember that the choice parts are next the head, the thin part is the next best, and the tail least esteemed. Make an incision along the back 9 to 10, and another from 1 to 2, and 3 to 4; cut the thickest part, between 10—2, for the lean. and 7—8 for the fat. When the fish is very thick, do not help too near the bone, as the flavor and colour are not so good.

Eels are usually cut into pieces about three inches long; and the thickest part being most esteemed, should be given first.

DIRECTIONS FOR CARVING JOINTS.

In assisting the more fleshy joints, such as beef, leg, or saddle of mutton, and fillet of veal, cut thin, smooth, and neat slices : taking care to pass the knife through to the bones of beef and mutton.

The carver would be saved much trouble, if the joints of carcass pieces of mutton, lamb, and veal, were divided by the butcher previous to cooking. If the whole of the meat belonging to each bone should be too thick, a slice may be taken off from between every two bones.

In assisting some boiled joints, as aitch-bone or round of beef, remove and lay aside a thick slice from the top, before you begin to serve.

Edge or Aitch-bone of Beef.

Cut off a slice three-quarters of an inch thick, from the upper part from 1 to 2; then help in long thin slices. The soft marrow-like fat lies below 3, at the back: the firm fat is to be cut in thin horizontal slices at 4. Before sending to table, the wooden skewers should be removed.

Part of a Sirloin of Beef.

There are two modes of helping this joint; either by carving long thin slices from 3 to 4, and assisting a portion of the marrowy fat, which is found underneath the ribs, to each person; or, by cutting thicker slices in the direction 1 to 2. When sent to table the joint should be laid down on the dish with the surface 2 uppermost.

Ribs of Beef are carved similar to the sirloin, commencing at the thin end of the joint, and cutting long slices, so as to assist fat and lean at the same time.

Round or Buttock of Beef.—Remove the upper surface in the same manner as for an aitch-bone of beef, carve thin horizontal slices of fat and lean, as evenly as possible. It requires a sharp knife and steady hand to carve it well.

Brisket of Beef

must be carved in the direction 1 and 2, quite down to the bone, after cutting off the outside, which should be about three-quarters of an inch thick.

Shoulder of Mutton

First cut down to the bone, in the direction of the line 1, and assist thin slices of lean from each side of the incision. The best fat is found at 2, and should be cut in thin slices in the direction of that line. Several delicate slices may be cut on either side of the line 3, and there are some nice bits on the under side, especially near the shank, and the flap. Some carve this joint by cutting long slices from the knuckle to the broad end, which is, in fact, an extension of line 3; it is not an economical way.

Leg of Mutton.

Wether mutton is esteemed most, and may be known by a lump of fat at the edge of the broadest part, as at 7. The finest slices are to be obtained from the centre, by cutting in the direction 1 to 2; and some very good cuts may be got off the broad end from 5 to 6. Some persons prefer the knuckle, which, though tender, is dry; the question should therefore be asked. By turning over the leg some excellent slices may be procured, especially when it is cold, by cutting lengthways, the same as carving venison. The cramp-bone is another delicacy, and is obtained by cutting down to the thigh-bone at 4, and passing the knife under it in a semi-circular direction to 3. The fat lies chiefly on the ridge 5. When sent to table, it should have a frill of paper or a knitted ornament round the knuckle; and if boiled, should lie on the dish as represented above, but should be turned over if roasted.

Haunch of Mutton consists of the leg and part of the loin, cut so as to resemble a haunch of venison, and is to be carved in the same manner.

Saddle or Chine of Mutton.—This is an excellent and elegant joint and should be carved in long thin smooth slices from the tail to the end, commencing close to the back-bone—a portion of fat being assisted with each slice, which must be taken from the sides. It is carved on both sides of the back-bone. Some carvers make an incision close to the back-bone throughout its length, and cut slices crossways from thence. If sent to table with the tail on, it may be removed by cutting between the joint.

Loin of Mutton is easily carved, as the bones are divided at the joints. Begin at the narrow end, and take off the chops; some slices of meat may be obtained between the bones, when the joints are cut through.

Fore Quarter of Lamb.

First separate the shoulder from the breast by passing the knife in the direction 3, 4, and 5. The body should be divided by an incision, as in 1, 2, so as to separate the ribs from the gristly part, and either may be assisted by cutting in the direction 6, 7 The shoulder is to be carved the same as mutton.

A Loin of Lamb, Leg of Lamb, and *Shoulder of Lamb* must be carved in the same manner as mutton, for which see directions.

Haunch of Venison.

First cut it across down to the bone in the line 1, 3, 2, then turn the dish with the end 4 towards you, put in the point of the knife at 3, and cut it down as deep as possible in the direction 3—4 after which, continue to cut slices parallel to 3—4 on the right and left of the line. The best slices are on the left of the line 3—4, supposing 4 to be towards you; and the fattest slices are to be found between 4 and 2.

Loin of Veal, should be jointed previous to being sent to table when the divisions should be separated with the carving-knife, and a portion of the kidney and the fat which surrounds it, given with each division.

A Breast of Veal Roasted,

should be divided into parts by an incision in the direction 1—2, then divide the brisket, or gristly part, into convenient pieces, as 3 —4, 5—6, and the ribs also, as 7 —8. The sweetbread, 9, may be divided into portions, or assisted whole; it is more economical however, to make a side dish of it

A Fillet of Veal,

is carved in a similar manner to a round of beef, in thin and smooth slices, off the top; some persons like the outside, therefore ask the question. For the stuffing, cut deep into the flap between 1—2, and help a portion of it to each person.

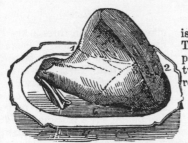

Knuckle of Veal,

is to be carved in the direction 1—2. The most delicate fat lies about the part 4, and if cut in the line 3—4, the two bones, between which the marrowy fat lies, will be divided.

A Roasted Pig.

The pig is seldom sent to table whole, but is divided by the cook, and served up as represented in the accompanying illustration. First divide the shoulder from the body on one side, and then the leg in the same manner; separate the ribs into convenient portions, and assist a little stuffing and gravy with each. If the head has not been divided, it must be done, and the brains taken out and mixed with the gravy and stuffing. The triangular piece of the neck is the most delcate part of the pig, the ribs the next best, and the ear is also regarded as a delicacy

Leg of Pork

,whether boiled or roasted, is carved the same. Commence about midway, between the knuckle and the thick end, and cut thin deep slices from either side of the line 1 to 2. For the seasoning in the roast leg, look under the skin at the thick end.

Hand of Pork.—Cut thin slices either across near the knuckle or from the blade-bone, the same as for a shoulder of mutton.

Loin of Pork is to be carved in the same manner as a loin of mutton

A Spare Rib of Pork is carved by cutting slices from the fleshy part, after with the bones should be disjointed and separated.

Ham

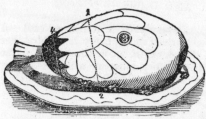

may be carved in three ways firstly, by cutting long delicate slices through the thick fat in the direction 1—2, down to the bone; secondly, by inserting the point of the carving-knife in the circle in the middle, taking out a piece as 3, and by cutting thin circular slices, thus enlarge the hole gradually, which keeps the meat moist; and thirdly, which is the most economical way, by commencing at the hock end 4—5, and proceeding onwards. When used for pies, the meat should be cut from the under side, after taking off a thick slice. It should be sent to table with a frill of white paper or a knitted ornament on the knuckle.

Half a Calf's Head Boiled

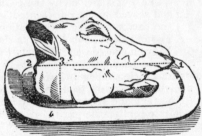

should be cut in thin slices from 1 to 2, the knife passing down to the bone. The best part in the head is the throat sweetbread, which is situated at the thick part of the neck 3, and should be carved in slices from 3 to 4, and helped with the other part. If the eye is wished for, force the point of the carving-knife down on one side to the bottom of the socket, and cut it quite round. The palate or roof of the mouth is esteemed a great delicacy; and some fine lean will be found on the lower jaw, and nice gristly fat about the ear. The brains and tongue are generally sent to table on a separate dish; the centre slice of the tongue is considered the best.

A Tongue

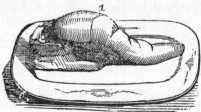

should be cut across, nearly through the middle, at the line 1, and thin slices taken from each side; a portion of the fat which is situated at the root of the tongue, being assisted with each.

POULTRY AND GAME.

All poultry should be well picked, every plug, or stub, removed, and the bird carefully and nicely singed with white paper. In drawing poultry, or game, care should be taken not to break the gall-bladder —as it would spoil the flavor of the bird by imparting a bitter taste to it, that no washing or any process could remove—nor the gut joining the gizzard, otherwise the inside would be gritty.

Observations on Carving.—The carving-knife for poultry and game is smaller and lighter than that for meat; the point is more peaked, and the handle longer.

In cutting up wild-fowl, duck, goose, or turkey, more prime places may be obtained by carving slices from pinion to pinion without making wings, which is a material advantage in distributing the bird when the party is large.

A GOOSE

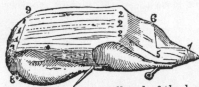

Turn the neck towards you, and cut two or three long slices on each side of the breast, in the lines 1—2, quite to the bone. Then remove the leg by turning the goose on one side, putting the fork through the small end of the leg-bone, and pressing it close to the body, which, when the knife is entered at 4, raises the joint; the knife is then to be passed under the leg, in the direction 4—5. If the leg hangs to the carcass at the joint 5, turn it back with the fork, and it will readily separate if young, but will require some strength if old. Take the wing off by putting the fork into the small end of the pinion, and press it close to the body; divide the joint at 3 with the knife, carrying it along as far as 4. When the leg and wing on one side are taken off, remove those on the other side.

To get at the stuffing, the apron must be removed by cutting in the line 6, 5, 7, and then take off the merry-thought in the line 8, 9. The neck-bones are next to be separated as in a fowl, and all other parts divided the same.

The best parts are the breast slices; the fleshy part of the wing, which may be divided from the pinion; the thigh-bone, which may be easily divided in the joint from the leg-bone; the pinion; and next, the side-bone. The rump is a nice piece to those who like it; and the carcass is preferred by some to other parts.

When assisting the stuffing, extract it with a spoon from the body through the aperture caused by removing the apron; mix it with the gravy, which should first be poured from the boat into the body of the goose, before any one is helped.

2*

TURKEY.

If the turkey is to be *boiled*, cut the first joint of the legs off; pass the middle finger into the inside, raise the skin of the legs and put them under the apron of the bird. Put a skewer into the joint of the wing and the middle joint of the leg, and run it through the body and the other leg and wing. The liver and gizzard must be put in the pinions, care being taken to open and previously remove the contents of the latter; the gall bladder must also be detached from the liver. Then turn the small end of the pinion on the back, and tie a packthread over the ends of the legs to keep them in their places.

If the turkey is to be *roasted*, leave the legs on, put a skewer in the joint of the wing, tuck the legs close up, and put the skewer through the middle of the legs and body; on the other side put another skewer in at the small part of the leg. Put it close on the outside of the sidesman, and push the skewer through, and the same on the other side. Put the liver and gizzard between the pinions, and turn the point of the pinion on the back. Then put, close above the pinions, another skewer through the body of the bird.

Carving.—The finest parts of a turkey are the breast, neck bones,

and wings; the latter will bear some delicate slices being removed. After the four quarters are severed, the thighs must be divided from the drum-sticks, which being tough, should be reserved till the last. It is customary not to cut up more than the breast, but if any more is required, to take off one of the wings; a thin slice of the force-meat, which is under the breast, should be given to each person, cutting in the direction from the rump to the neck.

FOWLS

Fowls must be picked very clean and the neck cut off close to the back. Take out the crop, and, with the middle finger, loosen the liver and other parts. Cut off the vent, draw it clean, and beat the breast bone flat with a rolling-pin.

If the fowl is to be *boiled*, cut off the nails of the feet, and tuck them down close to the legs. Put your finger into the inside, and raise the skin of the legs; then cut a hole in the top of the skin, and put the legs under. Put a skewer in the first joint of the pinion, and bring the middle of the leg close to it; put the skewer through the middle of the leg, and through the body, and then do the same on the other side. Open the gizzard, remove the contents, and wash well; remove the

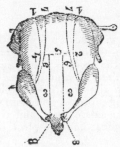

Boiled Fowl.

gall-bladder from the liver. Put the gizzard and the liver in the pinions, turn the points on the back, and tie a string over the tops of the legs, to keep them in their proper places.

If the fowl is to be *roasted*, put a skewer in the first joint of the pinion, and bring the middle of the leg close to it. Put the skewer through the middle of the leg, and through the body, and do the same on the other side. Put another skewer in the small of the leg, and through the sidesman; do the same on the other side, and then put another through the skin of the feet which should have the nails cut off.

Carving.—A fowl is cut up in the same way whether roasted or boiled. We have illustrated the method of carving upon the boiled fowl. Fix the fork in the middle of the breast at 5, take off the wing in the direction 1—2, dividing the joint at 1. Lift up the pinion with your fork, and draw the wing towards the leg, which will separate the fleshy part better than by the knife; and between the leg and the body at 3 to the bone as far as the joint;

then give the knife a sudden twist, and the joint will yield if the bird is young; repeat this on the other side, and then take off the merrythought in the line 2—5—4 by passing the knife under it towards the neck; now remove the neck-bones by passing the knife in at 7 under the long broad part of the bone in the line 7—6; then lifting it up, and breaking off the end of the shorter part of the bone, which cleaves to the breast-bone. Divide the breast from the back, by cutting through the tender ribs on each side, from the neck quite down to the vent; turn up the back, press the point of the knife about half way between the neck and rump, and on raising the lower end it will separate easily. Turn the rump from you, take off the sidesmen by forcing the knife through the rump-bone, in the lines 5—8, and the whole fowl is completely carved.

The prime parts of a fowl, whether roasted or boiled, are the wings, breast, and merry-thought; and next to these, the neck-bones and side-bones; the legs are rather coarse—of a boiled fowl, however, the legs are rather more tender than a roasted one; of the legs of a fowl the thigh is the better part, and therefore when given to any one should be separated from the drum-stick, which is done by passing the knife underneath, in the hollow, and turning the thigh-bone back from the leg-bone

PARTRIDGE.

Carving.—This bird is cut up in the same manner as a fowl, only on account of the smallness, the merry-thought is seldom divided from the breast. The wings must be taken off in the lines 1—2, and the merry-thought, if wished, in the lines 3—4. The prime parts are the wings, breast, and merry-thought. The wing is considered best, and the tip of it is esteemed the most delicate piece of the whole.

DUCK.

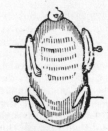

Carving.—Remove the legs and wings as directed before for a goose, and cut some slices from each side of the breast. The seasoning will be found under the apron, as in the other bird. If it is necessary, the merry-thought, &c., can be detached in the same manner as when carving a fowl.

Every kind of wild-fowl must be carved the same as a duck.

Back of Duck.

PIGEON.

If for *roasting*, cut off the toes, cut a slit in one of the legs, and put the other through it. Draw the leg tight to the pinion, put a skewer through the pinion legs, and body, and with the handle of the knife break the breast flat. Clean the gizzard, put it under one of the pinions, and turn the points on the back.

If for *boiling or stewing*, cut the feet off at the joint, turn the legs, and stick them in the sides, close to the pinions. If for a *pie*, they must be done in the same manner.

Carving.—There are three methods of carving them : 1st, as a chicken ; 2nd, by dividing them down the middle ; and 3rd, dividing them across, which is done by fixing the fork at 1, and entering the knife just before it, then cutting in the lines 1—2 and 1—3. The lower part is considered the better half

WOODCOCK, PLOVER, AND SNIPE

If these birds are not very fresh, great care must be taken in picking them, as they are very tender to pick at any time; for even the 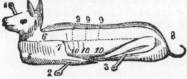 heat of the hand will sometimes take off the skin, which will destroy the beauty of the bird. When picked clean, cut the pinions in the first joint, and with the handle of a knife beat the breast bone flat. Turn the legs close to the thighs, and tie them together at the joints. Put the thighs close to the pinions, put a skewer into the pinions, and run it through the thighs, body, and other pinion. Skin the head, turn it, take out the eyes, and put the head on the point of the skewer, with the bill close to the breast.

These birds must never be drawn.

Carving.—Woodcocks and plovers are carved the same as a fowl, if large; but cut in quarters if small. Snipes are cut in halves. The head is generally opened in all.

RABBIT

Run a skewer through the two shoulders, at 2; another through the head at one, or pass it into the mouth and through the body, to keep the head in its place; two others should be passed through the roots of the ears to keep them erect; and another through the legs at 3. The inside of the ears should be singed out with a hot poker before roasting, and the eyes extracted with a fork. Many people let a rabbit soak in cold water all night before dressing, but a few hours is quite sufficient to extract the blood.

Carving.—Insert the point of the knife inside the shoulder at 6, and divide all the way down to the rump, on both sides, in the line 6, 7, 8, which will separate the rabbit into three pieces. Sever the shoulders in the direction 5, 6, 7, and the legs in a similar manner; as the latter is too large for one person in a large one, it should be divided from the thigh. Now behead it, cut off the ears close to the roots, and divide the upper from the lower jaw; then place the former on a plate, put the point of the knife into the forehead, and divide it through the centre down to the nose. Cut the back into several small pieces in the lines 9—10, and proceed to assist, giving some stuffing, (which is found below 10,) and gravy to each person. This can only be done easily when the animal is young; if old, it must be cut up as follows:—Cut off the legs and shoulders first, and then cut out long narrow slices on each side of the back-bone in the direction 7—8; then divide the back-bone into three or more parts, and behead as usual.

In conclusion, we may observe, that all printed directions must fail without constant practice, yet with practice, and due attention to the rules we have laid down, we doubt not that many of our readers will speedily become good carvers

SOUPS AND BROTHS.

GENERAL REMARKS.—The chief art in making good soup lies in the judicious blending of the different flavors, so that nothing shall predominate.

The scum should be taken off before the soup boils, or it will not be clear. All the fat is to be taken off.

Simmer very softly. If soup be suffered to boil quickly, the goodness of the meat can never be extracted.

Put the meat into cold water; let it be long on the fire before it comes to a boil; allow about two tablespoonfuls of salt to a gallon of soup, if it have many vegetables; less if the vegetables be few.

If the water waste, and more is to be added, use boiling water. Cold or lukewarm water will spoil the soup.

Keep the pot in which your soup is boiling closely covered, or the strength will fly off with the steam.

Soup will be as good the second day as the first, if heated to the boiling point. It should never be left in the pot, but should be turned into a dish or shallow pan, and set aside to get cold. Never cover it up, as that will cause it to turn sour very quickly.

Before heating a second time, remove all the fat from the top. If this be melted in, the flavor of the soup will certainly be spoiled.

Thickened soups require nearly double the seasoning used for thin soups or broth.

Soups are the substance of meat infused in water by boiling, and are of many different kinds, but may be divided into two classes, namely, *brown* and *white*. The basis of brown soups is always beef, while the basis of white soups is generally veal. Broths are preparations of soup, but more simple in their nature, and usually containing some kind of vegetables or matter for thickening, as rice, barley, &c. Soups of every description should be made of sound fresh meat and soft water. It is a general rule to allow a quart of water for every pound of meat; also to boil quickly at first, to make the scum rise, which is assisted by adding a little salt; and after skimming, to simmer gently.

To make Brown or Gravy Soup.—Take a shin or piece of the rump of beef, and break it in several places. Cut the beef from the bones; take out part of the marrow, and lay it on the bottom of the pot If there be no marrow, use butter. Then lay in the meat and bones to brown. Turn the whole when browned on one side, and take care it does not burn. When it is thoroughly browned, add a pint of cold water to draw the juice from the meat, also a little salt; and in a quarter of an hour after, fill in the quantity of cold water which may be requisite. Now add the vegetables, as, for instance, two carrots, a turnip, and three or four onions, all sliced; also a stalk of celery, some sweet herbs, with some whole black pepper. Let the soup boil slowly for from four to five hours, after which take it off, and let it stand a little to settle. Then skim off the fat, and put it through a hair sieve to clear it. The soup, if cleared, may now be either served or set aside for after use. It should have a clear bright look, with a brownish tinge. Frequently, it is made the day before using, in order that it may be effectually skimmed of fat. In such a case, it is heated again before serving. On some occasions, it is served with a separate dish of toasted bread cut in small squares.

The meat which has made the soup, is supposed to be divested of nearly all its nourishing qualities; but where thriftiness is consulted, it may form an agreeable stew, with vegetables, a little ketchup, and pepper and salt.

Brown Soup, made as above directed, forms what is called *stock*, that is, a foundation for every other soup of the brown kind, also as a gravy for stews where richness is required.

Beef or Mutton Soup.—Boil very gently in a closely covered saucepan, four quarts of water, with two table-spoonfuls of sifted bread raspings, three pounds of beef cut in small pieces, or the same quantity of mutton chops taken from the middle of the neck; season with pepper and salt add two turnips, two carrots, two onions and one head of celery, all cut small; let it stew with these ingredients 4 hours, when it will be ready to serve.

Cheap Broth for a Large Family.—Put a cupful of pearl barley into a pot with three quarts of cold water, and let it boil; then put in two pounds of neck of mutton; boil it gently for an hour, taking care to skim it occasionally, and watch it to prevent it boiling over. Then put in one grated carrot and two turnips, cut in small squares; an onion or two, sliced thin, or a leak, and two or three pieces of carrot and turnip, uncut. Some persons add the half of a small cabbage, chopped small, boil for an hour longer, have some bits of stale bread cut into fingers laid in the bottom of your tureen, pour the soup over it and send to table.

Broth made in an hour.—Cut into small pieces one pound of beef or veal. Put it into a saucepan, with a carrot, an onion, a slice of lean bacon, and half a glass of water; let it simmer for a quarter of an hour, then pour over it a pint of boiling water, add a little salt, let it boil three-quarters of an hour, and strain it through a sieve.

Mutton Broth.— This is an excellent broth for invalids, being of a very mild nature, and particularly efficacious to those whose stomachs have been rendered tender by much medicine. The best parts of mutton for making broth are either the scrag end of the neck or the chump end of the loin, which should be put into a clean saucepan with cold water in the proportion of a quart of water to every pound of meat. Throw in a little salt and skim it well as it comes to a boil; then set it aside that it may simmer very gently; slice in an onion and two turnips; let it stew for two hours, and just before you take it up, chop up a few sprigs of parsley very fine, and put into the broth, first taking out the mutton. Toast some bread in thin slices, and cut it in small squares into a bason; pour the broth over it and serve the meat in a dish; the turnips may be strained dry and served plain, or mashed up with a little butter, pepper, and salt.   Some prefer to thicken the broth with pearl barley.   If for a sick person, omit the herbs and vegetables.

White Soup.—Take a good knuckle of veal, or 2 or 3 short shanks boil it in 4 quarts of water about 4 hours, with some whole white pepper, a little mace, salt, 2 onions, and a small piece of lean ham strain it, and when cold take off all the fat and sediment; beat up 6 yolks of eggs, and mix them with a pint of cream; then pour the boiling soup upon it.   Boil the cream before putting it in the soup.

Family Soups.—Take 2 lbs. of lean beef, cut into small pieces, with one quarter lb. of bacon, 2 lbs. of mealy potatoes, 3 oz. of rice, carrots, turnips, and onions sliced, and cabbage.   Fry the meat, cabbage, and onions, in butter or dripping, the latter being the most savory; and put them into a gallon of water, to stew gently over a slow fire for 3 hours putting in the carrots at the same time, but the turnips and rice only time enough to allow of their being well done; and mashing the potatoes, which should be then passed through a cullender: season only with pepper and salt: keep the vessel closely covered.   It will make 5 pints of excellent soup.

Or.—To any quantity or kind of broth add whatever vegetables may be in season, and stew them gently till quite tender.   Then strain the soup; thicken it with flour and water, to be mixed gradually while simmering; and, when that is done, and seasoned to your taste, return the vegetables to the soup, and simmer for an hour.

Beef Broth.—Take a leg of beef, cut it in pieces; put it into a gallon of water; skim it; put in two or three blades of mace, some parsley, and a crust of bread; boil it till the beef and sinews are tender. Toast bread and cut into dice; put it in a dish; lay in the beef, and pour on the broth.

Plain Calf's Head Soup.—Boil the head in just enough water to cover it; when tender, remove the bones, cut the meat in small pieces and season with sweet-herbs, cloves, pepper and salt.   Put all back into the pot with the liquor, and thicken it with a little batter; stew gently for an hour, and just as you dish it up add a glass or two of sherry wine and the yolks of a few eggs boiled hard.

Mock Turtle Soup—Take a calf's head, the skin having been scalded and the hair scraped off clean, wash it thoroughly; take out the brains and boil them separately till done enough.   Put the head into a pot with more water than will cover it.   Skim it frequently till it boils, and let it boil for an hour, but very gently.   Take it out, and when cool cut the meat into pieces of about an inch square. Scrape and cut the tongue in the same manner. Lay all these pieces aside, then put into the water in which the head was boiled, about three or four pounds of leg of beef and a knuckle of veal—the meat cut small and the bones broken. Add four or five onions, a carrot and turnip, sliced, a small bunch of sweet-herbs, and some whole black pepper. Boil all together slowly, for four or five hours, then strain it and let it cool, when take off the fat. Now melt a lump of butter in a stewpan, put to it two handful of flour, and let it brown, stirring it all the time. Add a little of the soup, and a few sprigs of parsley. Boil this for a quarter of an hour, strain it through a sieve, put it, with the pieces of meat, into the soup, with the brains pounded, and boil all together for an hour. Add half a teacupful of ketchup, the juce of a lemon, cayenne pepper, and salt, to taste, also four glasses of sherry, and when dished in a tureen, put in two dozen of force-meat balls, and the same quantity of egg-balls, which are made as follows :—

Egg Balls.—Boil four or five eggs till they are quite hard. Take out the yolks and beat them in a mortar, with salt and cayenne pepper. Make this into a paste with the white of egg. Roll the paste into balls the size of small marbles. Roll them in a little flour and fry them in butter, taking care they do not break.

Force-meat Balls.—Cut half a pound of veal and half a pound of suet' fine, and beat them in a mortar. Have a few sweet-herbs shred fine ; dried mace beaten fine ; a small nutmeg grated ; a little lemon-peel cut very fine ; a little pepper and salt, and the yolks of two eggs ; mix all these well together, then roll them in little round balls ; roll them in flour and fry them brown. If for white sauce, put them in a little boiling water, and boil them for a few minutes, but do not fry them.

Pigeon Soup.—Take eight good pigeons ; cut up two, and put them on with as much water as will make a large tureen of soup, adding the pinions, necks, gizzards and livers of the others ; boil well and strain ; season the whole pigeons within with mixed spices and salt, and truss them with their legs into their belly. Take a large handful of parsley, young onions, and spinach ; pick and wash them clean, and shred small ; then take a handful of grated bread, put a lump of butter about the size of a hen's egg in a frying-pan, and when it boils throw in the bread, stirring well until it becomes a fine brown color. Put on the stock to boil, add the whole pigeons, herbs, and fried bread, and when the pigeons are done enough, dish up with the soup.

Soup a la Julienne, or Vegetable.—Cut various kinds of vegetables in pieces, celery, carrots, turnips, onions, &c., and having put two ounces of butter in the bottom of a stew-pan, put the vegetables on the top of the butter, together with any others that may be in season stew or fry them over a slow fire, keeping them stirred, and adding a little of the stock occasionally; soak small pieces of crust of bread in the remainder of the broth or stock, and when the vegetables are nearly stewed, add them, and warm the whole up together.

Cauliflower Soup.—Pick some small cauliflowers, cut them in pieces put them into a saucepan with a piece of butter, and brown them moisten them with water, and season. Add toasted slices of bread which soak in the soup, and let it simmer until the whole is dissolved together. Then serve.

Peas Soup.—This is an excellent soup, if well made, and is one of the cheapest soups that can be put on the table, for it may be formed of cold meat or marrow bone, or, what is cheaper still, merely water, or the liquor in which any piece of mutton, lamb, or veal, has been boiled. We give the following two recipes for making it :—

Peas Soup with Meat or Bones.—Take a good marrow bone, or the bones of cold roast beef; a slice or shank of ham may be added, if the flavor be liked. Break the bones, and put them in the pot with four quarts of cold water. According to the thickness and quantity required, take two or three pounds of the best split peas, and put them among the cold water and bones; add to this two carrots, two turnips, half a dozen small onions, a stalk of celery cut in pieces, a bunch of thyme, and some whole black pepper. Let all this boil for two hours, stirring frequently, as the soup is very apt to burn. When the peas are quite soft and broken down take the soup off, and put it through a sieve, into another pot; rub it well through until the pulp be mixed with the soup. Add salt melted amongst a little water, and boil the soup again for a few minutes. When to be served, cut a slice of toasted bread into small square pieces, and put in the tureen with the soup

Peas Soup without Meat or Bones.—Put two pounds or pints of peas in five quarts of water. Boil for four hours; then add three or four large onions, two heads of celery, a carrot and a turnip, all cut up; and season with salt, to taste. Boil for two hours longer. If the soup become two thick, add a little water. The peas may be boiled the evening before being used, and the longer they boil, the smoother and more mellow the soup will be; but do not put in the vegetables until the day the soup is to be used. By this plan the soup does not require straining.

Clam Soup.—Take forty or fifty clams, and wash and scrub the outside of the shells till they are perfectly clean. Then put them into a pot with just sufficient water to keep them from burning. The water must boil hard when you put in the clams. In about a quarter of an hour the shells will open, and the liquor run out and mix with the water, which must be saved for the soup, and strained into a soup-pot, after the clams are taken out. Extract the clams from their shells, and cut them up small. Then put them into the soup-pot, adding a minced onion, a saucer of finely chopped celery, or a table-spoonful of celery seed, and a dozen blades of mace. No salt, as the clam-liquor will be quite salt enough. If the liquid is not in sufficient quantity to fill a large tureen, add some milk. Thicken the soup with two large table-spoonfuls of fresh butter rolled in flour. Let it boil a quarter of an hour or twenty minutes. Just before you take it from the fire, stir in, gradually, the beaten yolks of five eggs; and then take up the soup and pour it into a tureen, the bottom of which is covered with toasted bread, cut into square dice about an inch in size.

Eel Soup.—Take 3 lbs. of small eels, and skin them; bone 1 or 2; cut them in very small pieces; fry them very lightly in a stew-pan with a bit of butter and a sprig of parsley. Put to the remainder 3 quarts of water, a crust of bread, 3 blades of mace, some whole pepper, an onion, and a bunch of sweet herbs; cover them close, and stew till the fish breaks from the bones; then strain it off; pound it to a paste, and pass it through a sieve. Toast some bread, cut it into dice, and pour the soup on it boiling. The soup will be as rich as if made of meat. 1-4th pint of cream or milk, with a tea-spoonful of flour rubbed smooth in it, is a great improvement.

Chicken Soup.—Cut up two large fine fowls, as if carving them for the table, and wash the pieces in cold water. Take half a dozen thin slices of cold ham, and lay them in a soup-pot, mixed among the pieces of chicken. Season them with a very little cayenne, a little nutmeg, and a few blades of mace, but no salt, as the ham will make it salt enough. Add a head of celery, split and cut into long bits, a quarter of a pound of butter, divided in two, and rolled in flour. Pour on three quarts of milk. Set the soup-pot over the fire, and let it boil rather slowly, skimming it well. When it has boiled an hour, put in some small round dumplings, made of half a pound of flour mixed with a quarter of a pound of butter; divide this dough into equal portions, and roll them in your hands into little balls about the size of a large hickory nut. The soup must boil till the flesh of the fowls is loose on the bones, but not till it drops off. Stir in, at the last, the beaten yolks of three or four eggs; and let the soup remain about five minutes longer over the fire. Then take it up. Cut off from the bones the flesh of the fowls, and divide it into mouthfuls. Cut up the slices of ham in the same manner. Mince the livers and gizzards. Put the bits of fowl and ham in the bottom of a large tureen, and pour the soup upon it.

Oyster Soup.—Take 2 quarts of oysters and drain them with a fork from their liquor; wash them in one water to free them from grit; cut in small pieces 2 slices of lean bacon, strain the oyster liquor and put in it the bacon, oysters, some parsley, thyme, and onions tied in a bunch as thick as the thumb, season with pepper and salt, if necessary; let it boil slowly, and when almost done, add a lump of butter as large as a hen's egg, rolled in flour, and a gill of good cream. It will take from 20 to 30 minutes to cook it.

FISH.

Fresh Cod, Boiled.—The thickness of this fish being very unequal, the head and shoulders greatly preponderating, it is seldom boiled whole, because in a large fish the tail, from its thinness in comparison to the upper-part of the fish, would be very much overdone. Whenever it is boiled whole, a small fish should be selected. Tie up the head and shoulders well, place it in the kettle with enough cold water to completely cover it; cast in a handful of salt. The fish if a small one, will be cooked in twenty minutes after it has boiled—if large it will take half an hour. When enough, drain it clear of the scum, remove the string; send it to table garnished with the liver, the smelt, and the roe of the fish scraped horse-radish, lemon-sliced, and sprigs of parsley.

The tail, when separated from the body of the fish, may be cooked in a variety of fashions. Some salt rubbed into it and hanging it two days, will render it exceedingly good when cooked. It may be spread open and thoroughly salted, or it may be cut into fillets, and fried.

If the cod is cooked when very fresh, some salt should be rubbed down the back and the bone before boiling—it much improves the flavor or, if hung for a day, the eyes of the fish should be removed, and salt filled in the vacancies. It will be found to give firmness to the fish and add to the richness of the flavor.

Salt Cod—Boiled.—Put the fish to soak over night, in warm water; set in a warm place. The next morning take it out of the water; scrape, and scrub it well with a hard brush; put it in a kettle of fresh cold water; bring it to the boiling point, and keep it at that heat until half an hour before dinner. Give it a good boil up; drain it well; and send to table with egg-sauce, or melted butter thickened with hard boiled eggs minced fine. Many people like salt pork cut in small square pieces, and fried brown, as a sauce for salt fish. It is sometimes also minced with potato, and warmed over when first sent to table.

Cod's Head and Shoulders.—Having selected a fine cod's head and shoulders, not severed, but in one piece, it must be cleaned, and left all night in salt. Skin it, and bind it with tape before dressing; then put it in a fish-kettle with the back turned over; pour in plenty of cold water, a little vinegar, and a handful of salt; heat it slowly, and boil t for half an hour; after that, the water must be drained from it across the top of the kettle; then place it with the back upwards, on the dish in which it is to be carried to table, after carefully removing the tapes; brush it over with beat egg, and then strew crumbs of bread, pepper, and salt, over it; finally, set it before a clear fire to brown. A rich sauce, made with beef-gravy instead of water, and highly seasoned with real cayenne pepper, salt, and catsup, must be poured in the dish around the fish.

Baked Cod-Fish.—Clean the piece of cod, and make a stuffing of bread-crumbs, parsley, and onions, chopped small, pepper and salt, a piece of butter moistened with egg; put this stuffing into the open part of the fish, and fix it in with skewers; then rub the fish over with beat egg, and strew crumbs of bread, pepper, and salt over it; stick also some bits of butter on it; set in a Dutch oven before the fire to bake; serve with melted butter or oyster-sauce

Fried Cod-Fish.—Take the middle or tail part of a fresh cod-fish, and cut it into slices not quite an inch thick, first removing the skin. Season them with a little salt and cayenne pepper. Have ready in one dish some beaten yolk of egg, and in another some grated bread-crumbs. Dip each slice of fish twice into the egg, and then into the crumbs—fry in butter and serve with gravy.

Stewed Cod-Fish.—Take a fine *fresh* cod, and cut into slices an inch thick, separated from the bones. Lay the pieces of fish in the bottom of a stew-pan: season them with a grated nutmeg; half a dozen blades of mace; a salt-spoonfull of cayenne pepper, and a small saucer-full of chopped celery, or a bunch of sweet-herbs tied together. Pour on half a pint of oyster liquor diluted with two wine glasses or a gill of water, and the juice of a lemon. Cover it close, and let it stew gently till the fish is almost done, shaking the pan frequently. Then take a piece of fresh butter the size of an egg; roll it in flour, and add it to the stew. Also, put in two dozen large fine oysters, with what liquor there is about them. Cover it again; quicken the fire a little, and let the whole continue to stew five minutes longer. Before you send it to table remove the bunch of sweet-herbs.

Cod-Fish Cakes.—Cold boiled fresh fish, or salt codfish, is nice minced fine, with potatoes, moistened with a little water, and a little butter put in, done up into cakes of the size of common biscuit, and fried brown in pork fat or butter.

Salmon—To Boil.—This fish cannot be too soon cooked after being caught; it should be put into a kettle with plenty of cold water and a handful of salt—the addition of a small quantity of vinegar will add to the firmness of the fish—let it boil gently; if four pounds of salmon. fifty minutes will suffice; if thick, a few minutes more may be allowed.

The best criterion for ascertaining whether it be done, is to pass a knife between the bone and the fish—if it separates readily, it is done; this should be tried in the thickest part; when cooked, lay it on the fish-strainer transversely across the kettle, so that the fish, while draining, may be kept hot. Place a fish-plate upon the dish on which the salmon is to be served, fold a clean white napkin, lay it upon the fish-plate, and place the salmon upon the napkin. Garnish with parsley.

Salmon—Broiled.—Cut the fish in slices from the best part—each slice should be an inch thick; season well with pepper and salt; wrap each slice in white paper, which has been buttered with fresh butter; fasten each end by twisting or tying; broil over a very clear fire eight minutes. A coke fire, if kept clear and bright, is best. Serve with butter, or tomato sauce.

Salmon—Roasted. Take a large piece of the middle of a very fine salmon, dredge well with flour, and while roasting, baste it with butter. Serve—garnished with lemon.

To bake Salmon.—Scale it, and take out the bone from the part to be dressed but fill up the cavity with forcemeat, and bind the piece with tape. Then flour it, rub it with yolk of egg, and put it into a deep baking-dish, covering it very thickly with crumbs of bread, chopped parsley, and sweet herbs, together with shrimps, if they can be got, and put into the covering a few small bits of fresh butter; place it in a Dutch oven, or, if already boiled and thus re-dressed, heat it only before the fire until browned.

To pickle Salmon.—Scale, clean, split, and divide into handsome pieces the salmon; place them in the bottom of a stew-pan, with just sufficient water to cover them. Put into three quarts of water one pint of vinegar, a dozen bay leaves, half that quantity of mace, a handful of salt, and a quarter ounce of black pepper. When the salmon is sufficiently boiled, remove it, drain it, place it upon a cloth. Put in the kettle another layer of salmon; pour over it the liquor which you have prepared, and keep it until the salmon is done. Then remove the fish, place it in a deep dish or pan, cover it with the pickle, which if not sufficiently acid, may receive more vinegar and salt, and be boiled forty minutes. Let the air be kept from the fish, and if kept for any length of time, it will be found necessary to occasionally drain the liquor from the fish; skim, and boil it.

To dry Salmon.—Cut the fish down, take out the inside and roe, rub the whole with common salt, after scaling it; let it hang 24 hours to drain. Pound 3 or 4 oz. of saltpetre, according to the size of the fish, 2 oz. of bay salt, and 2 oz. of coarse sugar; rub these, when mixed well, into the salmon, and lay it in a large dish or tray 2 days; then rub it well with common salt, and in 24 hours more it will be fit to dry; wipe it well after draining. Hang it either in a wood chimney or in a dry place, keeping it open with 2 small sticks. Dried salmon is eaten broiled in paper. and only just warmed through, egg-sauce and mashed potatoes with it; or, it may be boiled, especially the bit next the head.

To pot Salmon.—Take a large piece, scale and wipe, but do not wash it; salt very well, let it lie till the salt is melted and drained from it, then season with beaten mace, cloves and whole pepper: lay in a few bay-leaves, put it close into a pan, cover it over with butter, and bake it; when well done, drain it from the gravy, put it into the pots to keep, and when cold cover it with clarified butter.

In this manner you may do any firm fish.

Mackerel Boiled.—Cleanse the fish thoroughly inside and out, remove the roe carefully, steep it in vinegar and water, and replace it; place the fish in water, from which the chill has been taken, and boil very slowly from fifteen to twenty minutes—the best criterion is to be found in the starting of the eyes and splitting of the tail—when that takes place the fish is done; take it out of the water *instantly*, or you will not preserve it whole. Garnish with fennel or parsley, and either chopped fine into melted butter serve up as sauce.

To bake Mackerel.—Open and cleanse thoroughly, wipe very dry, pepper and salt the inside, and put in a stuffing composed of bread crumbs finely powdered, the roe chopped small, parsley, sweet herbs, very few of the latter; work together with the yolk of an egg, pepper and salt to taste, sew it in the fish, place the latter in a deep baking dish, dredge it with flour slightly, add a little cold fresh butter in small pieces, put them into an oven, and twenty or thirty minutes will suffice to cook them. Send them in a hot dish to table, with parsley and butter.

Broiled Mackerel.—Prepare by boiling a short time a little fennel, parsley and mint; when done take it from the steaks, and chop all together fine, mix a piece of butter with it, a dust of flour, pepper and salt; cut your fish down the back and fill it with this stuffing; oil your gridiron and oil your fish; broil then over a clear slow fire.

Another.—Empty and cleanse perfectly, a fine and very fresh mackerel, but without opening it more than is needful; dry it well, either in a cloth, or by hanging it in a cool air until it is stiff; make with a sharp knife, a deep incision the whole length of the fish, on either side of the back bone, and about 1-2 an inch from it, and with a feather put in a little Cayenne and fine salt, mixed with a few drops of good salad oil, or clarified butter. Lay the mackerel over a moderate fire upon a well heated gridiron, which has been rubbed with suet; loosen it gently should it stick, which it will do unless often moved: and when it is equally done on both sides, turn the back to the fire. About 30 minutes will broil it well.

To broil Mackerel.—Clean and split them open; wipe dry; lay them on a clean gridiron, rubbed with suet, over a very clean slow fire; turn; season with pepper, salt, and a little butter; fine-minced parsley is also used.

Mackerel, with Brown Butter.—Broil the fish like the preceding Dish it up; put some butter into the frying-pan; fry it in some parsley and pour the whole upon the mackerel; then warm in the pan a spoon ful of vinegar, some salt and pepper, which pour als: upon the fish, and serve hot.

Broiled Shad.—Empty and wash the fish with care, but do not open it more than is needful ; fill it with force meat and its own roe ; then sew it up, or fasten it securely with very fine skewers, wrap it in a thickly-buttered paper, and broil it gently for an hour over a charcoal fire. Serve it with caper sauce, or with Cayenne vinegar and melted butter.

To fry Shad.—Clean the fish, cut off the head, and split it down the back ; save the roe and eggs when taking out the entrails. Cut the fish in pieces about 3 inches wide, rinse each in cold water, and dry on a cloth ; use wheat flour to rub each piece. Have ready hot salted lard and lay in the fish, inside down, and fry till of a fine brown, then turn and fry the other side. Fry the roe and egg with the fish.

Baked Shad.—Make a force-meat of fine bread crumbs and cold ham —mince fine ; season with pepper, salt, and sweet marjoram ; bind with sweet milk on the yolk of an egg ; fill the inside of the fish with the stuffing, reserving a portion to rub the outside ; after having rubbed over the shad with the beaten yolk of an egg, lay the fish in a deep pan, put a little water in the bottom, add a glass of Port wine and a piece of butter, mixed with flour. A large shad will take an hour to bake. Pour the gravy over it, and send to the table—garnished with slices of lemon.

To pickle Shad.—Be sure that the fish are newly caught, for no other will be likely to keep. Soak them two hours in cold water ; scale ; cut off the heads, and open them through the back. If, after removing the intestines, you take out the back-bone, the fish will be more likely to keep sweet. As you scale lay them in fresh, cold water, and let them lie an hour, to soak out the blood. While this is doing prepare a pickle in a following manner: To every twenty-five shad allow one peck of rock salt, half fine, half coarse, a pound of sugar, and two ounces of saltpetre. Put a layer of coarse salt in the bottom of the barrel, then a layer of the fish previously well rubbed with a mixture of the sugar, fine salt and saltpetre, dissolved in a little water, the remainder of which should be diffused through the whole, as you thus proceed, until they are all in. Lay the fish with the skin-side down. Prepared in this way they will keep a year. Soak well before cooking.

To bake a Shad, Rock-fish or Bass.—Clean the fish carefully, sprinkle it lightly with salt and let it lie a few minutes ; then wash it, season it slightly with Cayenne pepper and salt, and fry it gently a light brown. Prepare a seasoning of bread crumbs, pounded cloves, parsley, Cayenne pepper and salt ; strew it over and in the fish ; let it stand an hour. Put it in a deep dish, and set it in the oven to bake ; to a large fish, put in the dish, the juice of a lemon made thick with loaf sugar, 1-2 tea-cupful of tomato ketchup ; to a small one allow in proportion the same ingredients ; baste frequently, and garnish with sliced lemon

To keep Shad Fresh without corning.—If you wish to keep a shad ever Sunday or longer—on bringing home immediately scald, clean, wash and split, washing dry. Cut off head and tail, spread the shad open on a dish, mix a large spoonful of brown sugar, teaspoonful of Cayenne pepper and a teaspoonful of salt; rub the mixture thoroughly over the inside of the fish, cover closely and set in a cold place until wanted for cooking—just before putting it on the gridiron, take a towel and wipe off the whole of the seasoning—then put it on a previously heated gridiron, over hot coals, and broil well, butter it and send to table, hot—where it can be re-seasoned to the taste of each person.

To boil Rock-Fish, Black-Fish, and Sea Bass.—Clean the fish with scrupulous care, particularly the back-bone, then lay the fish into the fish-kettle and cover it with cold water, strewing in a handful of salt and a small pinch of saltpetre, if you have it, and place it over a moderate fire, scum carefully and let it boil very gently until done, then drain and dish it nicely—garnish with hard boiled eggs cut in slices—celery or anchovy sauce or plain melted butter is most suitable for these fish.

Baked Rock-Fish and Bass.—Having the fish well cleaned, score with deep gashes, and lard with slices of salt pork. Make a stuffing of bread-crumbs, seasoned with butter, green summer-savoury and sage cut fine with the scissors, pepper, salt, and, if you like, other spices. Fill the body of the fish with stuffing. Sew up, bringing it into a curve; lay it in a deep dish, or dripping pan, on slices of salt pork; pour over a tea-cupful of sweet, rich cream, and bake in an oven heated for bread, from forty to fifty minutes.

Bass, black-fish, and shad, are delicious cooked in the same way.

Stewed Rock-Fish.—Take a large rock-fish, and cut it in slices near an inch thick. Sprinkle it *very slightly* with salt, and let it remain for half an hour. Slice very thin a dozen large onions. Put them into a stew-pan with a quarter of a pound of fresh butter, cut into bits. Set them over a slow fire, and stir them continually till they are quite soft, taking care not to let them become brown. Black-fish and bass are equally good cooked this way.

To souse Rock-Fish.—Boil the fish with a little salt in the water until it is thoroughly cooked. Reserve part of the water in which it was boiled, to which add whole pepper, salt, vinegar, cloves, allspice, and mace, to your taste; boil it up to extract the strength from the spice; and add the vinegar after it is boiled. Cut off the head and tail of the fish, and divide the rest in several portions. Put it in a stone jar, and when the fish is quite cold, pour the liquor over it. It will be fit to use in a day or two, and will keep in a cold place two or three weeks. **3**

Haddock.—Boil, or broil with stuffing as under, having salted them a day.

To dry Haddock. Choose them of two or three pounds weight, take out the gills, eyes, and entrails, and remove the blood from the back-bone. Wipe them dry, and put some salt into the bodies and eyes. Lay them on a board for a night; then hang them up in a dry place, and after three or four days, they will be fit to eat; skin and rub them with egg, and strew crumbs over them. Lay them before the fire, and baste with butter until brown enough. Serve with egg-sauce.

To bake Haddock, &c.—The scales should be scraped off, but the tail and head must not be removed, though the spinal bone should be taken out, and the body stuffed with any approved forcemeat.

Whitings.—To boil Whitings.—Having scraped, cleaned, and wiped them, lay them on a fish-plate, and put them into water at the point of boiling; throw in a handful of salt, 2 bay-leaves and plenty of parsley, well washed and tied together; let the fish *just simmer* from 5 to 10 minutes, and watch them closely that they may not be overdone. Serve parsley and butter with them, and use in making it the liquor in which the whitings have been boiled. Just simmered from 5 to 10 minutes.

Sturgeon.—To dress fresh Sturgeon.—Cut slices, rub egg over them, then sprinkle with crumbs of bread, parsley, pepper, salt; fold them in paper and broil gently.
Sauce; butter, anchovy, and soy.

To roast Sturgeon.—Put it on a lark-spit, then tie it on a large spit; baste it constantly with butter; and serve with good gravy, an anchovy, a squeeze of Seville orange or lemon, and a glass of sherry.

To boil Halibut.—Take a small halibut, or what you require from a large fish. Put it in the fish-kettle, with the back of the fish undermost, cover it with cold water, in which a handful of salt, and a bit of saltpetre the size of a hazel nut, have been dissolved. When it begins to boil, skim it carefully, and then let it just simmer till it is done. 4 lbs. of fish will require nearly 30 minutes, to boil it. Drain it, garnish with horseradish or parsley—egg sauce or plain melted butter, are served with it.

Halibut.—Stewed.—Put into a stew-pan half a pint of fish broth, a table-spoonful of vinegar, and one of mushroom, ketchup, two good sized onions, cut in quarters, a bunch of sweet herbs, add one clove of garlic, and a pint and a half of water; let it stew an hour and a quarter, strain it off clear, put into it the head and shoulders of a fine halibut, and stew until tender; thicken with butter and flour, and serve.

To bake Pike.—Scale it, and open as near the throat as you can then stuff it with the following: grated bread, herbs, anchovies, oysters, suet, salt, pepper, mace, half a pint of cream, four yolks of eggs mix all over the fire till it thickens, then put it in the fish, and sew it up, butter should be put over it in little bits ; bake it. Serve sauce of gravy, butter, and anchovy.

To boil Perch.—First wipe or wash off the slime, then scrape off the scales, which adhere rather tenaciously to this fish ; empty and clean the insides perfectly, take out the gills, cut off the fins, and lay the perch into equal parts of cold and of boiling water, salted as for mackerel : from 8 to 10 minutes will boil them unless they are very large. Dish them on a napkin, garnish them with curled parsley, and serve melted butter with them.

Trout.—Scale, gut, clean, dry, and flour, fry them in butter until they are a rich clear brown, fry some green parsley crisp and make some plain melted butter, garnish when the trout are dished with the crisped parsley and lemon cut in slices ; the butter may be poured over the fish, but it is most advisable to send it in a butter tureen.

To bake Trout.—Cover the bottom of a small oval paper form with a few very thin slices of fat bacon, cut down the back some nicely-washed small trout, and having removed the bones, lay the fish open, flat upon the bacon ; sprinkle with chopped parsley, pepper, salt, a little mace, and 2 cloves finely pounded. Bake 30 minutes in a quick oven, and serve in paper.

To boil Trout.—They should be wiped dry with a coarse towel, rubbed from head to tail, and boiled whole, putting them into cold water mixed with a small quantity of vinegar, into which should be also put some scraped horse-radish ; let them boil gradually for about 20 to 30 minutes, according to size, and take care not to break the skin ; serve with plain melted butter.

Boiled Eels.—Use small ones ; stew with plenty of parsley, in very little water. The parsley must be served as well. For sauce, use parsley chopped fine, and melted butter with it.

Fried Eels.—Any size will be suitable for this purpose, but if small, tie head and tail together ; dip into a mixture of eggs and bread crumbs, and then fry.

To Broil Eels.—The same process may be adopted by merely changing the frying-pan for the gridiron, and wrapping the eels in buttered paper ; but, if thought proper, the bread-crumbs and herbs may be omitted, as well as the envelope of paper, and the eel merely brushed over with the yolk of egg. Turn them frequently, and take them up when quite brown.

Fried Flounders.—Clean the fish; dry them in a cloth sprinkle with salt; and dredge them well with flour. Put them in hot fat, and fry brown, turning them carefully, so as not to break the fish.

Trout, perch, carp, or any small fish, may be fried in the same way. Or if you wish to make them richer, dip each in the beaten yolk of egg, and flour, or bread-crumbs, before frying.

Chowder.—Take some thin pieces of pork and fry brown; cut each fish into several pieces, place them by layers in your pork fat, sprinkle a little pepper and salt—add cloves, mace, sliced onions; lay on bits of fried pork, if you choose, and crackers soaked in cold water; then turn on water just sufficient to cover them, and put on a heated bake-pan lid. After stewing about twenty minutes, take up the fish, and mix two tea-spoonfuls of flour with a little water, and stir it into the gravy, adding a little pepper and butter ketchup and spices also, if you choose. Cod and bass make the best chowder. Clams and black-fish are tolerably good. The hard part of the clam should be cut off and rejected.

SMALL FISH.

Sun Fish, Frost Fish, Smelts, Minnows, or other small fish, must be well cleaned and dried, and shaken in a floured cloth, and may then be fried either with a little butter, or in boiling fat. Or they may be first dipped in egg, and sprinkled with fine bread crumbs.

They will scarcely take more than two minutes to make them of a nice brown color, when they are done. Let them be drained on a hair sieve, before the fire, till they are pretty free from fat.

SHELL FISH.

Lobsters to be eaten cold.—Procure the lobsters alive. Hen lobsters are the best, as they have spawn in and about them. Put them in boiling water, along with some salt, and boil from half an hour to three quarters of an hour, or more, according to the size. When done, take them out of the water and wipe the shells. Before they are quite cold, rub the shells with a buttered cloth. Take off the large claws, and crack the shells carefully, so as not to bruize the meat. Split the body and tail lengthwise, in two pieces. This may be done with a knife. Place the whole of the pieces ornamentally on a dish and garnish with parsley.

. Crabs to be boiled same way.

Lobster Salad.—Take one or two heads of white heart lettuce; they should be as fresh as possible; lay them in spring water for an hour or two; then carefully wash them, and trim off all the withered or cankered leaves; let them drain awhile, and dry them lightly in a clean napkin.

From the Lobster.—Take out the coral, or red meat, and mince the remaining parts very fine. Mash the coral fine, with the yolks of four hard boiled eggs, a little sweet oil, mustard, pepper, and salt, all mixed well, and moistened with vinegar; incorporate this mixture thoroughly with the meat; put it on a dish; sprinkling the whole with lettuce minced very fine.

To make a Crab Pie.—Procure the crabs alive, and put them in boiling water, along with some salt. Boil them for a quarter of an hour or twenty minutes, according to the size. When cold, pick the meat from the claws and body. Chop all together, and mix it with crumbs of bread, pepper and salt, and a little butter. Put all this into the shell, and brown before the fire. A crab shell will hold the meat of two crabs.

Minced Crab.—Remove the meat, mince small, and place in a saucepan with a wineglassful of wine, pepper and salt, nutmeg, cayenne, and two tablespoonfuls of vinegar. Let it stew for ten minutes; melt a piece of butter the size of a hen's egg with an anchovy and the yolks of two eggs; beat up and mix well; stir in with the crab, and add sufficient stale bread crumbs to thicken; garnish with thin toast, cut with a pastry leaf-cutter, or with the claws and parsley.—Lobster may be done thus.

Oysters Stewed.—Take a pint of oysters, gently simmer them in their own strained liquor. Beard them and add a quarter of a pint of cream; season with pounded mace, cayenne, and salt; add two ounces of butter and a dessert spoonful of flour, then simmer for a short time. Lay the oysters in the dish upon a piece of toast, and pour the sauce over. The cream may be omitted, if thought proper.

To fry Oysters.—Make thick batter of eggs, milk, flour, pepper, and salt, and dip the oysters singly in the batter; after which, fry them in dripping or lard in a frying-pan, being careful that they do not stick together. A sauce may be used, composed of the liquor of the oysters, thickened with flour and butter, and seasoned with Cayenne pepper and a little ketchup.

Mussels may be dressed in the same manner, but several are dipped together in the batter, by means of a spoon, and so fried together.

Broiled Oysters.—Take the largest and finest oysters. See that your gridiron is very clean. Rub the bars with fresh butter, and set it over a clear steady fire, entirely clear from smoke; or on a bed of bright hot wood coals. Place the oysters on the gridiron, and when done on one side, take a fork and turn them on the other; being careful not to let them burn. Put some fresh butter in the bottom of a dish. Lay the oysters on it, and season them slightly with pepper Send them to table hot.

For Oyster Patties.—Make some rich puff-paste and bake it in very small tin patty-pans. When cool, turn them out upon a large dish. Stew some large fresh oysters with a few cloves, a little mace and nutmeg, some yolk of egg boiled hard and grated, a little butter and as much of the oyster liquor as will cover them. When they have stewed a little while, take them out of the pan, and set them away to cool. When quite cool, lay two or three oysters in each shell of puff-paste.

To pickle Oysters. Wash four dozen of the largest oysters you can get in their own liquor, wipe them dry, strain the liquor off, adding to it a desert-spoonful of pepper, two blades of mace, a table-spoonful of salt, if the liquor be not very salt, three of white wine, and four of vinegar.—Simmer the oysters a few minutes in the liquor, then put them in small jars, and boil the pickle up, skim it, and when cold, pour over the oysters : cover close.

Oyster Pie.—Line a deep dish with a fine puff paste. Lay a plate of the same size over the top, to support the upper crust, which you must lay on, and bake, before the oysters are put in, as in the time required for cooing the paste, they would be over-done. While the paste is baking, prepare the oysters. Take their liquor, and having strained, thicken it with the yolk of egg, either boiled hard and grated, or beaten thoroughly, and a piece of butter rolled in bread-crumbs. Season with mace and nutmeg. Stew the whole five minutes, or till well done. Carefully remove the cover from the pie ; take out the plate ; put in the oysters, with their gravy ; replace the cover, and send to table, hot. If you like the pie dryer, put in only half the liquor. You may make flowers of strips of the paste, and garnish the crust.

Clams.—To boil clams wash them well from the loose sand, put but very little water in the pot, as soon as the shells open they are done, take them out, wash each one carefully in the liquor, cut off the black portions, lay them in a saucepan with some of the liquor, a piece of butter rolled in flour, with a little pepper and vinegar, heat scalding hot, and serve.

Clams Roasted.—Lay them on a gridiron or hot coals till the shells open—then take them out and preserve the liquor to serve with them.

To boil Soft-shell Clams. —When the shells are washed clean, put the clams in a pot with the edges downwards ; pour a quart of boiling water over them to open the shells ; set them over the fire for nearly an hour. When they are done the shells will be wide open ; then take them out of the shells, trim off the black skin that covers the hard part ; put them in a stew-pan with some of their own liquor, to which add butter, pepper, and salt. Let them boil a few minutes.

To fry Hard-shell Clams.—Take the large sand clams ; wash them in their own liquor , beat well the yolks of 4 eggs with a little pepper and a table-spoonful of fine flour. Dip in the clams and fry them in butter a light brown.

Clam Fritters.—Take 50 soft shell clams cut the hard stem off, and examine it carefully to see that none of the shell remains on it. wash them well and chop fine, then beat up 2 eggs, add a pint of milk, a little nutmeg, and as much saleratus as will cover a shilling, add flour enough to make a batter, put in the clams, stir well together and fry in lard or drippings.

Clam Pie.—Take a sufficient number of clams to fill a large pie-dish when opened. Make a nice paste in the proportion of a pound of fresh butter to two quarts of flour. Paste for shell-fish, or meat, or chicken pies should be rolled out double the thickness of that intended for fruit pies. Line the sides and bottom of your pie-dish with paste. Then cover the bottom with a thin beef-steak, divested of bone and fat. Put in the clams, and season them with mace, nutmeg, and a few whole pepper-corns. No salt. Add a spoonful of butter rolled in flour, and some hard-boiled yolks of eggs crumbled fine. Then put in enough of the clam-liquor to make sufficient gravy. Put on the lid of the pie (which like the bottom crust should be rolled out thick,) notch it handsomely, and bake it well. It should be eaten warm.

MEATS.

The best apparatus for roasting is the tin oven—or tin kitchen, as it is generally called; and the next to this is the open baker, with reflectors, to set before the fire ; but *roasting*, in most families of these days, has degenerated into *baking*.

In roasting the sirloin or any piece of beef, if an open fire is used precaution must be taken to prevent its being too close to the fire where there is much fat, and it is desired to preserve it from being cooked before the lean, it may be covered with clean white paper skewered over it ; when it is nearly done the paper should be removed, a little flour dredged over it, and a rich frothy appearance will be obtained The joint should be served up with potatoes and other vegetables ; the dish should be garnished round the edge with horse-radish scraped into thin curls. This receipt will suffice for all the other roasting parts of beef.

Sirloin weighing ten pounds, will take two hours and a half to roast it. Rather more time must be allowed in cold than in hot weather about twenty minutes to the pound is a safe rule.

Rump of Beef.—This is one of the most juicy of all the joints of beef. As it is too large to serve whole, generally, cut as much from the chump end to roast as will make a handsome dish. Manage it as the sirloin. When boned and rolled into the form of a fillet of veal, it requires more time.

Beef A-La-Mode.—Remove the bone from a round, or any piece of beef that will stew well. Make a stuffing of bread crumbs seasoned with sweet marjoram, pepper, mace, nutmeg, and onions, or shalots chopped fine. Mix this together with two eggs well beaten, and add, if you like, some chopped salt pork. Fill the place from which the bone was taken with this seasoning, rubbing what is left over the out-side of the meat. Bind, and skewer it well, to secure the stuffing. You may stick whole cloves into the meat here and there; or lard it with fat pork. Cover the bottom of your stewpan with slices of ham, or salt pork; and having put in the meat, lay slices of the ham, or pork, over it. Pour in about a pint of water; cover the pan closely, and bake in an oven six, seven, or eight hours, according to the size of the piece. Add, if you like, a tea-cupful of port wine, and the same of mushroom ketchup to the gravy; but it is very good without wine This dish is best cold.

Dripping.—Roast beef yields a dripping, which is a valuable article in the economy of the kitchen. It should be removed from the pan beneath the meat before it becomes overheated, or scorched by the fire, leaving sufficient for basting. Dripping is prepared for future use in the following manner:—As taken hot from the dripping-pan, pour it in to boiling water, when all particles of cinder or other improper matter will fall to the bottom, and leave the pure fat on the surface. Col-lect these cakes of fat, and by heating them in a jar, placed in a sauce-pan of boiling water, the whole will become a solid mass, and may be thus put aside for use. This process not only purifies dripping, but gives it a clear white colour. A little salt must be infused, to assist in preserving it.

Beef Heart Roasted.—Wash thoroughly, stuff with forcemeat, send to table as hot as it is possible with currrant jelly sauce; it will take about forty minutes roasting, but this depends upon the fire.

Beef Heart.—Let it be thoroughly well cooked, and the skin remov-ed. Wipe it daily with a clean cloth, stuff it with veal stuffing; roast two hours and a quarter. Make a brown gravy, as for hare; and serve with the gravy and currant jelly.

The most pleasant way to the palate of dressing this dish, is to roast the heart rather less than two hours, let it get cold, cut it in pieces, and jug it the same as hare.

To Stew Kidneys.—Cut the kidneys into slices; wash them, and dry them with a clean cloth; dust them with flour, and fry them with butter until they are brown. Pour some hot water or beef gravy in-to the pan, a few minced onions, pepper, and salt, according to taste, and add a spoonful or two of mushroom ketchup before dishing. Min-ced herbs are considered an improvement to many tastes—cook slowly ten or fifteen minutes.

To Stew a Piece of Beef or Make Beef Bouilli.—Take a piece of beef; the brisket or rump, or any other piece that will become tender. Put a little butter in the bottom of the stew-pan, and then putting in the meat, partially fry or brown it all over. Then take it out and lay two or three skewers at the bottom of the pan; after which replace the meat, which will be prevented from sticking to the pan by means of the skewers. Next put in as much water as will cover the meat. Stew it slowly with the pan closely covered, till done, with a few onions if required. Two hours are reckoned enough for a piece of six or eight pounds. When ready, take out the meat, and thicken the gravy with a little butter and flour. Cut down into handsome shapes a boiled carrot and turnip, and add them to the liquor; season with pepper, and salt, and a little ketchup. Boil all together for a few minutes, and serve in a hash dish.

To Mince Beef.—Shred the underdone part fine, with some of the fat; put it into a small stew-pan, with some onion or shalot (a very little will do), a little water, pepper, and salt; boil it till the onion is quite soft; then put some of the gravy of the meat to it, and the mince. Do not let it boil. Have a small hot dish with sippets of bread ready, and pour the mince into it, but first mix a large spoonful of vinegar with it: if shalot-vinegar is used, there will be no need of the onion nor the raw shalot.

To Hash Beef. Do it the same as in the last receipt, only the meat is to be in slices, and you may add a spoonful of walnut-liquor or ketchup.

Observe, that it is owing to *boiling* hashes or minces that they get hard. All sorts of stews, or meat dressed a second time, should be only simmered; and this last only hot through.

Steaks—Broiled.—They should not be cut more than three quarters of an inch thick, or they will not be done well through. Let the gridiron be perfectly clean, and heat and grease it before laying on the meat. Set it over a bed of clear bright coals, and when done on one side turn the steaks with tongs made for the purpose, or a knife and fork. In a quarter of an hour they will be well done; or if you like them rare, ten or twelve minutes will be sufficient. Pour off into a dish, and save all the gravy that accumulates while boiling; and when done lay the steaks in a dish, and season to your taste with pepper, salt, and butter. Serve hot.

To fry Beef-Steaks.—Cut the steaks as for broiling, and, on being put into the pan, shift and turn them frequently. Let them be done brown all over, and placed in a hot dish when finished. Gravy may be made by pouring a little hot water into the pan after the steaks are out, and the fat poured away, with a little pepper, salt, ketchup. and flour. The gravy so formed is to be poured into the dish with the steaks. Serve to table immediately.

3*

If onions be required along with the dish, cut them in thin slices and fry them till they are soft. They should be fried after the steaks and merely with part of the fat in which the beef has been fried.

Beef-steak Pie.—A good common paste for meat-pies, and which is intended to be eaten, is made as follows: Three ounces of butter, and one pound of flour, will be sufficient for one dish. Rub the butter well amongst the flour, so as to incorporate them thoroughly. If the butter be fresh, add a little salt. Mix up the flour and butter with as much cold water as will make a thick paste. Knead it quickly on a board, and roll it out flat with a rolling pin. Turn the dish upside down upon the flattened paste, and cut or shape out the piece required for the cover. Roll out the parings, and cut them into strips. Wet the edges of the dish, and place these strips neatly round on the edges, as a foundation for the cover. Then take some slices of tender beef mixed with fat; those from the rump are the best. Season them with pepper and salt, and roll each slice up in a small bundle, or lay them flat in the dish. Put in a little gravy or cold water, and a little flour for thickening. Then, after putting in the meat, lay the cover on the dish, pressing down the edges closely to keep all tight. If any paste remain cut or stamp it into ornaments, such as leaves, and place these as a decoration on the cover.

On taking pies from the oven, and while quite hot, the crust may be glazed with white egg and water beat together, or sugar and water, laid on with a brush.

To dress Beef Tongues.—To dress them, boil the tongue tender, it will take five hours; always dress them as they come out of the pickle, unless they have been very long there, then they may be soaked, three or four hours in cold water, or if they have been smoked, and hung ong, they should be softened by lying in water five or six hours; they should be brought to a boil gently, and then simmer untill tender; when they have been on the fire about two hours, and the scum removed as it rises, throw in a bunch of sweet herbs of a tolerable size, it will improve the flavour of the tongue.

Tripe.—May be served in a tureen, stewed with milk and onion till tender. Melted butter for sauce.

Or fry it in small bits dipped in butter.

Or stew the thin part, cut into bits, in gravy · thicken with flour and butter, and add a little ketchup.

Or fricassee it with white sauce.

Soused Tripe.—Boil the tripe, but not quite tender; then put it into salt and water, which must be changed every day till it is all used. When you dress the tripe, dip it into a batter of flour and eggs, and fry it of a good brown.

VEAL.

To Keep Veal.—The first part that turns bad of a leg of veal, is where the udder is skewered back. The skewer should be taken out, and both that and the part under it wiped every day, by which means it will keep good three or four days in hot weather. Take care to cut out the pipe that runs along the chine of a loin of veal, as you do of beef, to hinder it from tainting. The skirt of a breast of veal is likewise to be taken off; and the inside of the breast wiped and scraped, and sprinkled with a little salt.

Leg of Veal.—Let the fillet be cut large or small as best suits the number of your company. Take out the bone, fill the space with a fine stuffing and let it be skewered quite round; and send the large side uppermost. When half roasted, not before, put a paper round the fat; and take care to allow a sufficient time, and put it a good distance from the fire, as the meat is solid: serve with melted butter poured over it.—You may pot some of it.

Knuckle of Veal.—As few people are fond of boiled veal, it may be well to leave the knuckle small, and take off some cutlets or collops before it is dressed; but as the knuckle will keep longer than the fillet, it is best not to cut off the slices till wanted. Break the bones, to make it take less room; wash it well, and put it into a sauce-pan with three onions, a blade of mace or two, and a few pepper-corns; cover it with water, and simmer till quite ready. In the mean time some macaroni should be boiled with it if approved, or rice, or a little rice-flour, to give it a small degree of thickness; but do not put too much. Before it is served, add half a pint of milk and cream, and let it come up either with or without the meat.

Shoulder of Veal.—Remove the knuckle and roast what remains, as the fillet; it may or may not be stuffed at pleasure; if not stuffed, serve with oyster or mushroom sauce; if stuffed, with melted butter.

To roast Veal.—The best parts of veal for roasting are the fillet, the breast, the loin, and the shoulder. The fillet and the breast should be stuffed, particularly the fillet; the stuffing to be composed of crumbs of bread, chopped suet and parsley, a little lemon peel, and pepper and salt, wet with an egg and a little milk. The piece should have a slow fire at first, and will require longer time to dress than beef or mutton. Let it be well basted with butter when there is not sufficient dripping from the joint. The gravy for roast veal is either the usual hot water and salt, or thin melted butter, poured over the meat.

To boil Calf's Head.—Clean it very nicely, and soak it in water, that it may look very white; take out the tongue to salt. and the brains to make a little dish. Boil the head extremely tender; then strew it over with crumbs and chopped parsley, and brown them ; or if liked better, leave one side-plain. Serve bacon and greens to eat with it.

The brains must be boiled, and then mixed with melted butter, scalded sage chopped, pepper and salt.

If any of the head is left, it may be hashed next day, and a few slices of bacon, just warmed and put round.

Cold calf's head eats well if grilled.

Minced Veal.—Cut cold veal as fine as possible, but do not chop it. Put to it a very little lemon-peel shred, two grates of nutmeg, some salt, and four or five spoonfuls of either a little weak broth, milk, or water ; simmer these gently with the meat, but take care not to let it boil, and add a bit of butter rubbed in flour. Put sippets of thin toasted bread, cut into a three-cornered shape round the dish

Veal Cutlets with fine Herbs.—Melt a piece of butter in the frying-pan ; put in the cutlets with salt, pepper, and some spice ; move them about in the butter for five minutes ; have ready some mixed herbs and mushrooms chopped finely ; sprinkle half over one side of the cutlets, and, when fried enough, turn and sprinkle them with the other half ; finish frying, and add the juice of a lemon ; set them round the dish with the seasoning in the centre.

French way of dressing a Shoulder of Veal—Cut the veal into nice square pieces or mouthfuls, and parboil them. Put the bone and trimmings into another pot, and stew them slowly a long time, in a very little water, to make the gravy. Then put the meat into the dish in which it is to go to table, and season it with a very little salt and cayenne pepper, the yellow rind of a large lemon grated, and some powdered mace and nutmeg. Add some bits of fresh butter rolled in flour, or some cold dripping of roast veal. Strain the gravy and pour it in. Set it in a hot dutch-oven, and bake it brown.

To roast Sweet-breads.—Sweet-breads should be soaked in warm water, and then blanched by being thrown into boiling water, boiled for a few minutes, and then put into cold water. They may then be larded and roasted or fried, and afterwards stewed in butter with crumbs of bread, and being of themselves rather insipid, they will be improved by a relishing sauce and by a large quantity of herbs in the braise. Skins of lemon put upon the sweet-breads while braising will heighten the flavor, and keep them white ; which is very desirable when sent to table with white sauce. The usual sauce with which they are served is butter and mushroom ketchup. They may be roasted in a dutch-oven.

Calves' Feet.—They should be very clean, boil them three hours, or until they are tender, serve them with parsley and butter.

Calf's Heart.—Stuff and roast precisely as beef heart. See page 56.

Calf's Liver roasted.—Wash and wipe it; then cut a long hole in it, and stuff it with crumbs of bread, chopped anchovy, herbs, a good deal of fat bacon, onion, salt, pepper, a bit of butter and an egg: sew the liver up; then lard it, or wrap it in a veal-cawl, and roast it.

Serve with a good brown gravy, and currant jelly.

Cutlets another way—Cut slices about three quarters of an inch thick, beat them with a rolling pin, and wet them on both sides with an egg: dip them into a seasoning of bread-crumbs, parsley, thyme, pepper, salt, and a little nutmeg grated; then put them into papers folded over, and boil them; and have in a boat melted butter with a little mushroom-ketchup.

Veal Olives.—Take some cold fillet of veal and cold ham, and cut them into square slices of the same size and shape, trimming the edges evenly. Lay a slice of veal on every slice of ham, and spread some beaten yolk of egg over the veal. Have ready a thin force-meat, made of grated bread-crumbs, sweet-marjoram rubbed fine, fresh butter, and grated lemon-peel, seasoned with nutmeg and a little cayenne pepper. Spread this over the veal, and then roll up each slice tightly with the ham. Tie them round securely with coarse thread or fine twine; run a bird-spit through them, and roast them well. For sauce, simmer in a small sauce-pan, some cold veal gravy with two spoonfuls of cream and some mushroom ketchup.

Calves' Tongues.—Wash them well, and put them in hot water for a short time, in order to take off the hard skin; lard them here and there with large pieces of bacon; put them in a saucepan so as to yield a little gravy, with two or three large onions and carrots. When the whole is well glazed, add some water, salt, a clove, and a sprig of thyme, and let it simmer very slowly for five hours. Just before serving, skim the sauce, thicken it with some flour; open each tongue in half, so that it forms a heart shape, and pour the sauce over; adding to it either some pickled gherkins sliced, or some mushrooms.

Calves' tongues may, moreover, be prepared like those of oxen.

Potted Veal.—This may be potted as beef, or thus:—pound cold veal in a mortar, work up with it in a powder mace, pepper, and salt, shred the leanest part of tongue very finely, or ham is sometimes used place in a jar or pot a layer of the pounded veal, and upon that a layer of the tongue, and continue alternately until the pot is full, seeing that every layer is well pressed down; pour over the top melted clarified butter. If it is desired, and which is frequently done, to marble the veal, cut the tongue or ham in square dice instead of shredding it, but care must be taken that they do not touch each other or the effect is destroyed.

Calves' Brains.—Wash them, remove the skin, and scald. Dry them well, fry them in butter, serve with mushroom sauce. Instead of this when cleaned and scalded, chop them finely, simmer them with mushrooms, onions, parsley, sage, and white sauce, season highly, serve with fried parsley.

Veal Pie.—Take about two pounds of veal from the loin, fillet, or any odd pieces you may have. Parboil enough to clear it of the scum. If it is to be done in a pot, make a very light paste according to directions for such purposes; roll it out rather thick; and having your pot well greased lay it round the sides, cutting out pieces to prevent thick folds, as the circle diminishes. Put in a layer of meat, with salt and pepper. Enrich with butter, or slices of salt pork, and dredge in a little flour. So proceed until you have put all in. Cover with paste, and cut a hole in the top for the escape of the steam. Pour in a portion of the water, in which the meat was boiled. Set it over a slow fire; watch that it does not burn; and if it get too dry, add more of the same water, through the hole in the top. If you wish the crust brown, cover the top with a heater or bake-pan cover. It will be done in an hour and a half.

If the pie is *baked* make a richer crust, in the proportion of a pound of butter to two pounds of flour; put it in a pan, in the same manner as above; notch the edges of the paste handsomely and bake about the same time.

MUTTON.

Roast Leg of Mutton.—Put the leg into an iron saucepan with enough cold water to cover it, let it come to a boil gently, parboil it by simmering only; have the spit or jack ready. and take it from the hot water and put it to the fire instantly; it will take from an hour to an hour and a half if large, and less time if small.

Shoulder of Mutton.—Must be well roasted and sent to table with skin a nice brown, it is served with onion sauce. This is the plainest fashion, and for small families the best.

Saddle of Mutton.—This joint like the haunch, gains much of its flavour from hanging for some period, the skin should be taken off, but skewered on again until within rather more than a quarter of an hour of its being done, then let it be taken off, dredge the saddle with flour, baste well. The kidneys may be removed or remain at pleasure, but the fat which is found within the saddle should be removed previous to cooking.

Neck of Mutton.—This dish is most useful for broth, but may be made a pleasant dish by judicious cooking. To send it to table merely boiled or baked is to disgust the partaker of it. When it is cooked as a single dish, first boil it slowly until nearly done, then having moistened a quantity of bread crumbs and sweet herbs, chopped very fine. with the yolk of an egg, let the mutton be covered with it, and placed in a Dutch or American oven before the fire, and served when nicely browned. The breast may be cooked in the same manner.

To boil a Leg of Mutton.—A leg of mutton should be kept four or five days before boiling. Before putting it into the pot, bend round the shank, cutting the tendon at the joint if necessary, so as to shorten the leg. Two hours of slow equal boiling will be sufficient for a good-sized leg of mutton. Some persons, to make the leg look white and tasteful, wrap it tightly in a cloth in boiling; but this spoils the liquor for broth. It is not safe to boil vegetables with a leg of mutton, as they are apt to flavour the meat. Dish the leg with a litttle of the liquor, placing the lower side uppermost, conveniently for carving. A good leg of mutton will yield sufficient gravy.

Turnips mashed or whole form the appropriate vegetable to be eaten with this dish.

Loin of Mutton Stewed.—Remove the skin, bone it, and then roll it, put it in a stewpan with a pint and a half of water, two dessert-spoonfuls of pyroligneous acid, a piece of butter, sweet herbs, and an onion or two; when it has stewed nearly four hours strain the gravy, add two spoonfuls of red wine, hot up and serve with jelly sauce.

Breast of Mutton.—May be stewed in gravy until tender, bone it, score it, season well with cayenne, black pepper, and salt, boil it, and while cooking skim the fat from the gravy in which it has been stewed, slice a few gherkins, and add with a dessert spoonful of mushroom ketchup; boil it, and pour over the mutton when dished.

Mutton Hashed.—Cut the remains of a cold leg or shoulder of mutton into thin slices, whether fat or lean; flour and pepper well and leave on the dish. Boil the bones, well broken up, with a few onions minced well, add some salt, a little mushroom ketchup and the hashed meat; warm over a slow fire, but do not let it boil; then add port wine and currant jelly, or omit, as you please. If the former, it will impart a venison flavour, if the latter method is adopted it will be plain.

To Dress Mutton Hams.—Soak the ham for five or six hours in cold spring water unless it has only recently been cured, then one hour will suffice; put it into cold water, boil gently; it will be done in two hours and a half. It is eaten cold.

To Boil a Sheep's Head.—Soak and wash the head in cold water taking care to remove all the splinters of the bones, and to clean the brains thoroughly of all the skin and blood. Put it into a saucepan, cover it with lukewarm water and a good spoonful of salt; let it boil very gently, skimming it well from time to time. When it has boiled about an hour, take off all the fat; and having cut up a good sized onion two turnips, a carrot, a small head of celery, and a sprig or two of parsley, put them into the broth with a little thyme and a crust of bread toasted brown; cover up the saucepan, and let the broth simmer gently for an hour and a half, when the head will be done. Serve it up with the brains chopped up in melted butter, poured over it, and turnips in another dish. Serve the broth, which will be excellent, in a tureen.

To Fry Mutton Chops.—They require to be cut in the same manner as for broiling, and may be dressed according to the preceding directions for steaks. None of the grease which flows from the chops is to be used along with them, and the whole must be poured away before preparing the gravy.

To Broil Mutton Chops.—Mutton-chops should not be broiled on too fierce a fire, otherwise the fat will cause the fire to flare, and the chops will be smoked and blackened. Pepper them and salt them the same as beefsteaks; but, unlike those, mutton chops require constant turning; they should not be overdone.

When they are done enough, lay them in a hot dish and sprinkle them with salt; they require no butter, the chops being sufficiently fat.

Irish Stew.—Put two pounds of breast of mutton into a pot, with a pint and a half of water and a pinch of salt; let it stew gently for an hour; then take off all the fat; take out the meat and cut it into small pieces; have ready four pounds of potatoes, pared and cut in halves; three or four good sized onions, peeled and sliced, and pepper and salt mixed in a cup. When you have taken the fat off the broth as closely as possible, put in a layer of potatoes; then sprinkle two or three pieces of meat with the pepper and salt, and lay them on the potatoes, then a layer of the sliced onions, then another layer of potatoes, one of mutton, then one of onions, and so on till the whole is in. Cover close and let it stew very gently for another hour, shaking it frequently that it may not burn.

To Broil Kidneys.—Split them through lengthways, and run an iron skewer through them to keep them flat; pepper them, and broil them over a clear fire. They should be lightly done. Serve them in a very hot dish, sprinkle them with salt. and put a bit of butter on each.

LAMB.

To Roast Lamb.—Lamb requires to be well roasted, as, if not sufficiently done, it will fail to acquire that delicate taste so peculiar to it. It is commonly dressed in quarters. Lamb should be well jointed or chopped by the butcher, as it is such a delicate sort of meat, that it becomes altogether disfigured, if the carver is compelled to hack and pull it in pieces. In roasting, baste with its own dripping, and after pouring off all the fat, serve it up in a hot dish with the gravy that remains after the fat is poured off. In serving up a fore-quarter, the cook should divide the shoulder neatly from the ribs, and after squeezing the juice of half a lemon on the ribs, cover the shoulder closely over again. It is usual to send up with lamb, mint-sauce in a tureen.

To Roast a Shoulder of Lamb (savoury).—Score the joint with cuts an inch deep, rub it over with butter first, then season it with pepper and salt, and sweet-herbs; rub over these the yolk of an egg, and roll it in bread-crumbs; roast it a light brown. When sufficiently cooked pour off the fat in the dripping-pan, and make a gravy of that which remains, seasoning with pepper and salt, tomato or mushroom-ketchup, the grated rind and juice of a lemon, thickened with a little flour. Put the lamb on a clean hot dish and pour the gravy over it.

To Boil a Leg of Lamb.—A leg of lamb is a delicate dish when nicely boiled. If whiteness is desirable, wrap it in a clean cloth; only the liquor will then be spoiled for broth. Boil one of five pounds gently for about an hour and a half. When you dish it, cut the loin into chops, fry them, and lay round it. Sauce, plain melted butter, or parsley and butter.

To Fry Lamb Chops.—Lamb chops may be either simply fried in the same manner as mutton chops, or dressed with egg and crumbs of bread (but with no parsley), as in the case of cutlets. Gravy made in the pan, as for fried steaks.

A very nice dish.—Take the best end of a neck of lamb, cut into steaks, and chop each bone so short as to make the steaks almost round. Egg, and strew with crumbs, herbs, and seasoning; fry them of the finest brown; mash some potatoes with a little butter and cream, and put them into the middle of the dish raised high. Then place the edge of one steak on another with the small bone upward all round the potatoes.

VENISON.

To keep Venison.—Keep the venison dry, wash it with milk and water very clean, and dry it with clean cloths till not the least damp remains; then dust pounded ginger over every part, which is a very good preventive against the fly. By thus managing and watching, it will hang a fortnight. When to be used, wash it with a little luke-warm water, and dry it. Pepper is likewise good to keep it.

Roast Venison.—A haunch of buck will take three hours and a half or three quarters roasting; doe, only three hours and a quarter. Venison should be rather under than over done.

Spread a sheet of white paper with butter and put it over the fat, first sprinkling it with a little salt; then lay a coarse paste on strong paper and cover the haunch, tie it with fine pack-thread, and set it at a distance from the fire, which must be a good one. Baste it often; ten minutes before serving take off the paste, draw the meat nearer the fire, and baste it with butter and a good deal of flour to make it froth up well.

Gravy for it should be put into a boat, and not into the dish (unless the venison has none,) and made thus:—Cut off the fat from two or three pounds of a loin of old mutton, and set it in steaks on a gridiron for a few minutes, just to brown one side; put them into a sauce-pan with a quart of water, cover close for an hour, and simmer it gently; then uncover it and stew till the gravy is reduced to a pint. Season with only salt.

Currant-jelly sauce must be served in a boat.

To prepare Venison for Pasty.—Take the bones out, then season and beat the meat, lay it into a stone jar in large pieces, pour upon it some plain drawn-beef gravy, but not a strong one; lay the bones on the top, then set the jar in a water-bath, that is, a saucepan of water over the fire, simmer three or four hours, then leave it in a cold place till next day. Remove the cake of fat, lay the meat in handsome pieces on the dish; if not sufficiently seasoned, add more pepper, salt, or pimento, as necessary. Put some of the gravy, and keep the remainder for the time of serving. If the venison be thus prepared, it will not require so much time to bake, or such a very thick crust as is usual, and by which the under part is seldom done through.

Venison Pasty.—A shoulder boned makes a good pasty, but it must be well beaten and seasoned, and the want of fat supplied by that of a fine well hung loin of mutton, steeped twenty-four hours in equal parts of ripe vinegar and port. The shoulder being sinewy, it will be of advantage to rub it well with sugar for two or three days. and when to be used, wipe it perfectly clean from it, and the wine.

A mistake used to prevail that venison could not be baked too much but, as above directed, three or four hours in a slow oven will be quite sufficient to make it tender, and the flavor will be preserved. Either in a shoulder or side, the meat must be cut in pieces, and laid with fat between, that it may be proportioned to each person without breaking up the pasty to find it. Lay some pepper and salt at the bottom of the dish, and some butter; then the meat nicely packed, that it may be sufficiently done, but not lie hollow to harden at the edges.

The venison bones should be boiled with some fine old mutton—of this gravy put half a pint cold into the dish, then lay butter on the venison, and cover as well as line the sides with a thick crust, but do not put one under the meat. Keep the remainder of the gravy till the pasty comes from the oven; put it into the middle by a funnel, quite hot, and shake the dish to mix well. It should be seasoned with pepper and salt.

To stew cold Venison.—Cut the meat in small slices, and put the trimmings and bones into a saucepan, with barely enough water to cover them. Let them stew two hours. Strain the liquor in a stew-pan; add to it some bits of butter rolled in flour, and whatever gravy was left of the venison. Stir in some currant jelly, and let it boil half an hour. Then put in the meat, and keep it over the fire long enough to heat it through, but do not let it boil.

Minced Venison, or Hash.—Chop up the meat in small pieces, put them by and make gravy with the remaining parts, or some veal or mutton broth will do. Add some butter rolled in flour, and flavor with currant jelly. Put in the venison, and let it simmer till perfectly warmed through.

PORK.

To roast Pork.—Pork requires a longer time in roasting than any of the preceding meats. When stuffing is to be used, it must be composed of chopped sage and onion, pepper and salt. The pieces should be neatly and well scored in regular stripes on the outer skin, to enable the carver to cut slices easily. Before putting to the fire, rub the skin with salad oil, to prevent its blistering, and baste very frequently. The basting may be done by rubbing it with a piece of butter in a muslin bag, when there is not enough of dripping. The gravy for pork may be the same as for other joints, hot water and salt poured over it on the dish. It is considered an improvement to have apple-sauce served in a small tureen, as it assists in overcoming the richness or lusciousness of the meat, and imparts a slight acidulous flavor.

To boil fresh Pork.—Take a flat blade-bone of country pork, take out the bone, and put veal stuffing in its place, wrap it in a clean cloth and put it in a saucepan of boiling water with a little salt; let it boil slowly for about an hour and a half, or an hour and three quarters, according to the size: it should, however, well be done. Serve it up with parsley and butter poured over it plentifully. This is a most rich, and at the same time a most delicate dish, equal to boiled fowl and pickled pork, which, indeed, it greatly resembles.

To Boil Pickled Pork.—Having washed and scraped it, put it into boiling water with the skin-side uppermost. If it be thin, a piece of four pounds will be done in less than an hour; a leg of eight pounds will take three hours. Pork should be done enough; but if boiled too fast or too long, it will become jelly. Keep the pot well skimmed, and send it to table with peas-pudding and greens. Some persons like carrots, parsnips also.

To Boil Bacon and Beans.—These must be boiled separately, otherwise the bacon will spoil the color of the beans. Soak the bacon for an hour or two in cold water, trim and scrape it as clean as possible, and put it into enough cold water to cover it: set it over slow fire, so that it will be half an hour before it comes to a boil; then skim it and let it boil gently till done. Two or three pounds will require an hour and a half after it boils; the hock or gammon, being thick, will require more time. When done enough, strip off the rind; and your beans in the meantime having been boiled and strained, put them into a deep dish, lay the bacon upon them, and send them to table, with parsley and butter in a boat.

To boil a Ham.—If the ham has been long cured, soak it in cold water for from twelve to twenty hours. Scrape it and put it into a large vessel to boil, with plenty of cold water, and let it simmer gently from three to four or five hours according to the size. A ham of twenty pounds will require four hours and a half. Skim the pot frequently to remove the grease as it rises. When done, strip off the rind, and strew bread-raspings over the top side, then set it before the fire, or in the oven, to dry and brown. Some persons prefer to bake a ham; it is then necessary, after soaking and scraping, to enclose it in a paste of flour and water before sending it to the oven.

To broil Ham.—Cut the ham about the third of an inch thick, and broil it very quickly over a brisk fire; lay it on a hot dish, pepper it, and put on it a good lump of butter.

Roast Pig.—Soak in milk some light bread, boil some sage and onions in plenty of water, strain it off and chop it very fine, press the milk from the bread, and then mix the sage and onion with pepper and salt, in the bread put the yolk of an egg to bind it a little, put this in the inside of the pig, rub the pig over with milk and butter, paper it, roast it a beautiful brown, cut off the head before it is drawn from the spit, and likewise cut it down the back and then you will not break the skin ; take out the spit, cut off the ears from the head, and crack the bone and take out the brains, put them in a stewpan with all the inside stuffing and a little brown sauce ; dish the pig, the back outside, and put the sauce in the middle, and some in a boat, the ears at each end.

Pig's Head Baked.—Let it be divided and thoroughly cleaned ; take out the brains, trim the snout and ears, bake it an hour and a half, wash the brains thoroughly, blanch them, beat them up with an egg, pepper and salt, and some finely cut or powdered sage, and a small piece of butter, fry them or brown them before the fire ; serve with the head.

Pig's Head Boiled.—This is a more profitable dish though not so pleasant to the palate : it should first be salted, which is usually done by the pork butcher ; it should be boiled an hour and a quarter ; it must boil gently or the meat will be hard ; serve with vegetables.

To fry Pork Chops.—Pork chops should be cut rather thin, and be thoroughly dressed. They may be either simply fried in the same manner as chops, or fried after being dipped in egg, and sprinkled with crumbs of bread, and sage and onion finely chopped. No gravy is expected with pork chops. If any sauce be used, it must be apple sauce.

Cheshire Pork Pie.—Take the skin of a loin of pork, and cut the loin into steaks, season with salt, pepper, and dried sage. Make a good crust, line the dish with it, and put in a layer of pork, then a layer of sliced pippins dipped in sugar, then another layer of pork, cover in the pie and bake in a moderate oven.

To fry Pork Sausages.—All sausages are fried alike, and require to be dressed very slowly. Before being put into the pan, they should be pricked in several places with a fine fork, to prevent their bursting by the expansion of the air within.

It is common in England to bring fried sausages to table neatly laid out on a flat dish of mashed potatoes. The sausages and potatoes are helped together. They may also be laid in links on toasted bread, and garnished with poached eggs around the dish.

Fried sausages are sometimes used for garnishing roast turkey.

To Pickle Pork—The quantities proportioned to the middlings of a pretty large hog, the hams and shoulders being cut off.

Mix, and pound fine, four ounces of saltpetre, a pound of coarse sugar, an ounce of sal-prunel, and a little common salt ; sprinkle the pork with salt, and drain it twenty-four hours : then rub with the above ; pack the pieces tight in a small deep tub, filling up the spaces with common salt. Place large pebbles on the pork, to prevent it from swimming in the pickle which the salt will produce. If kept from air it will continue very fine for two years.

Sausages.—Chop fat and lean of pork together ; season it with sage pepper, and salt, and you may add two or three berries of allspice : *half fill* hogs' guts that have been soaked and made extremely clean : or the meat may be kept in a very small pan, closely covered ; and so rolled and dusted with a very little flour before it is fried. Serve on stewed red cabbage, or mashed potatoes put in a form, brown and garnish with the above ; they must be pricked with a fork before they are dressed or they will burst.

Head Cheese.—Take some tongues, feet, and head of tender pork— and any fragments of meat on hand, clean, and scrape as for souse, boiling till the meat falls off, chop it small flavor to taste, mixing it in well, put in a forcer or cheese hoop, and press, with plate on top and a weight over ; in two or three days it will be ready for use.

Soused Pig s Feet.—Take the ears, feet, and upper part of the head, scrape clean, boil until the meat is tender, take it up ; so flavor properly —and put into pure vinegar, spice as you like. Put it in a jar and keep closely covered. Tripe can be pickled in the same way.

Jelly of Pig's Feet and Ears.—Clean and prepare as in the last article, then boil them in a very small quantity of water till every bone can be taken out ; throw in half a handful of chopped sage, the same of parsley, and a seasoning of pepper, salt, and mace, in fine powder ; simmer till the herbs are scalded, then pour the whole into a melon form.

GENERAL DIRECTIONS FOR CURING MEATS, &C.

To make a Pickle that will keep for years, for Hams, Tongues, or Beef, if boiled and skimmed between each parcel of them.

To two gallons of spring-water put two pounds of coarse sugar, two pounds of bay and two pounds and a half of common salt, and half a pound of saltpetre, in a deep earthen glazed pan that will hold four gallons, and with a cover that will fit close. Keep the beef or hams as long as they will bear, before you put them into the pickle ; and sprinkle them with coarse sugar in a pan, from which they must drain. Rub the hams, &c. well with the pickle, and pack them in close ; putting as much as the pan will hold, so that the pickle may cover them. The pickle is it not to be boiled at first. A small ham may lie fourteen days, a large one three weeks ; a tongue twelve days, and beef in pro portion to its size. They will eat well out of the pickle without dry ing. When they are to be dried, let each piece be drained over the pan; and when it will drop no longer, take a clean sponge and dry it thoroughly. Six or eight hours will smoke them, and there should be only a little sawdust and wet straw burnt to do this; but if put into a chimney, sew them in coarse cloth and let them hang a week.

To cure Hams.—Hang them a day or two; then sprinkle them with a little salt, and drain them another day; pound an ounce and a half of saltpetre, the same quantity of bay-salt, half an ounce of sal-prunel, and a pound of the coarsest sugar. Mix these well; and rub them into each ham every day for four days, and turn it. If a small one turn it every day for three weeks; if a large one, a week longer; but do not rub after four days. Before you dry it, drain and cover with bran. Smoke it ten days.

Another way.—Choose the leg of a hog that is fat and well-fed; hang it as above; if large, put to it a pound of bay salt, four ounces of saltpetre, a pound of the coarsest sugar, and a handful of common salt, all in fine powder, and rub it thoroughly. Lay the rind downwards, and cover the fleshy parts with the salts. Baste it as often as you can with the pickle, the more the better. Keep it four weeks, turning it every day. · Drain it, and throw bran over it; then hang it in a chimney where wood is burned, and turn it sometimes for ten days.

Another way.—Hang the ham, and sprinkle it with salt as above: then rub it every day with the following, in fine powder: half a pound of common salt, the same quantity of bay-salt, two ounces of saltpetre, and two ounces of black pepper, mixed with a pound and a half of treacle. Turn it twice a day in the pickle, for three weeks. Lay it into a pail of water for one night, wipe it quite dry, and smoke it two or three weeks.

Another way that gives it a high flavor.—When the weather will permit, hang the ham three days; mix an ounce of saltpetre, with a quarter of a pound of bay-salt, the same quantity of common salt, and also of coarse sugar, and a quart of strong beer; boil them together, and pour them immediately upon the ham; turn it twice a day in the pickle for three weeks. An ounce of black pepper, and the same quantity of allspice, in fine powder, added to the above, will give still more flavor. Cover it with bran when wiped, and smoke it from three to four weeks, as you approve: the latter will make it harder and give it more of the flavor of Westphalia. Coarse wrap, if to be smoked where there is a strong fire.

A method of giving a still higher flavor.—Sprinkle the ham with salt, after it has hung two or three days; let it drain; make a pickle of a quart of strong beer half, a pound of treacle, an ounce of coriander seeds, two ounces of juniper-berries, an ounce of pepper, the same quantity of allspice, an ounce of saltpetre, half an ounce of sal-prunel, a handful of common salt, and a head of shallot, all pounded or cut fine. Boil these all together a few minutes, and pour them over the ham : this quantity is for one of ten pounds. Rub and turn it every day, for a fortnight ; then sew it up in a thin linen bag, and smoke it three weeks. Take care to drain it from the pickle, and rub it in bran before drying.

To cure Mutton Ham.—Cut a hind-quarter of good mutton into the shape of a ham, pound 1 oz. of saltpetre, with 1 lb. of coarse salt, and 4 oz. of brown sugar, rub the ham well with this mixture, taking care to stuff the whole of the shank well with salt and sugar, and let it lie a fortnight, rubbing it well with the pickle every 2 or 3 days ; then take it out and press it with a weight for 1 day ; smoke it with sawdust for 10 or 15 days, or hang it to dry in the kitchen. If the ham is to be boiled soon after it has been smoked, soak it 1 hour, and if it has been smoked any length of time, it will require to be soaked several hours. Put it on in cold water, and boil it gently 2 hours.

Hog's Lard.—Melt it with great care in a jar, put into a kettle of water, set on the fire to boil, adding to the lard a sprig of rosemary' while melting ; then run it into small clean bladders.

Suet and lard keep better in tin than in earthen vessels ; suet may be kept for a year, if chopped, packed in tin, and covered with treacle.

POULTRY.

To Roast a Turkey.—Having picked, drawn, and singed the turkey, truss it according to previous directions for trussing fowls. Stuff the breast with rich veal stuffing, adding a little sausage-meat ; sew up the neck. Cover the breast with buttered paper to preserve it from scorching, and roast it to a fine brown. Baste it well with butter ; and a little while before it is done remove the paper and allow the breast to brown. A good-sized turkey will require roasting from an hour and a half to two hours. You must have plenty of good gravy in the dish, and garnish with lemon. Serve with bread-sauce.

To Boil a Turkey.—A boiled turkey is a most delicate and excellent dish, and requires to be dressed with extreme care. Clean the turkey from feathers and stumps, and singe off the hairs, taking care not to blacken the skin. Draw and wipe it inside with a clean dry cloth ; cut off the legs at the first joint ; draw out the sinews ; then pull down the skin and push the legs inside ; cut the head off close to the body, leaving the skin long, and draw out the craw. Make a good veal-stuffing and put it into the breast, leaving sufficient room for the stuffing to swell ; then draw the skin of the breast over the opening and sew it neatly across the back, so that when the turkey is brought to table no sewing will appear. Place the gizzard in one wing and the liver in the other ; turn the wing on the back and fix them to the sides with a skewer; wrap it in a cloth dredged with flour, and put i, into a pot of warm water, in sufficient quantity to keep the turkey always covered. Skim it while boiling. A small, young turkey will not take more than an hour and a half to boil it; a large one about two hours and a half. When done place it in a hot dish, and pour a little sauce over the breast. Send up oyster-sauce, or parsley and butter, in a tureen. Some cooks make the stuffing of chopped bread and butter oysters, cream, and the yolks of eggs.

Pulled Turkey.—Divide the meat of the breast by pulling instead of cutting; then warm it in a spoonful or two of white gravy, and a little cream, grated nutmeg, salt, and a little flour and butter; do not boil it. The leg should be seasoned, scored, and broiled, and put into the dish with the above round it. Cold chicken does as well.

Turkey Patties.—Mince some of the white part, and with grated lemon, nutmeg, salt, a very little white pepper, cream, and a very little bit of butter warmed, fill the patties.

To Roast Goose.—Pick, draw, and singe the goose well. Cut off its head and neck. Take off the feet and legs at the first joint; also, take off the wings at the first joint. The portions of the legs and wings that are left are skewered to the sides. Stuff with chopped sage and onion, and crumbs of bread, with pepper and salt. The skin of the neck must be tied securely, to prevent the gravy from running out. Paper the breast for a short time. A goose does not require so much basting as fowl or turkey, for it is naturally greasy. It will require from two hours to two hours and a half in roasting. It ought to be thoroughly done. Serve with gravy sauce and apple sauce. The liver, gizzard, head, neck, feet, and the pinions of the goose, form what is termed the *giblets*, and compose a good stew or pie.

Green-Goose Pie.—Bone two young green geese, of a good size; but first take away every plug, and singe them nicely. Wash them clean; and season them high with salt, pepper, mace, and allspice. Put one inside the other; and press them as close as you can, drawing the legs inwards. Put a good deal of butter over them, and bake them either with or without crust; if the latter, a cover to the dish must fit close to keep in the steam. It will keep long.

To Stew a Goose.—Truss the goose as for boiling, cover it with bacon and tie it up; cover the sauce-pan with bacon; put in a sprinkle of sweet herbs: a carrot cut in dice and two bay leaves; lay in the goose and giblets; cover with bacon; moisten with as much stock as will cover the goose; let it boil, cover with buttered paper and a close cover, and set it on a hot hearth, with fire over it; give it an hour and a half. Serve it with onion or apple sauce.

4

To Roast Ducks.—Pick, draw, and singe them. Cut off the head, dip the feet in boiling water to remove the yellow skin; truss them plump, turning the feet flat upon the back. Stuff the same as goose, and serve with gravy and apple sauce. An hour will roast a duck. Green peas, usually accompany roast duck.

Stewed Duck with Green Peas.—Put a deep stew-pan on the fire with a piece of fresh butter; singe the duck; flour it, and put it in the stewpan to brown, turning it two or three times; pour out the fat, but let the duck remain in the pan; put to it a pint of good gravy, a pint of peas, two lettuces cut small, a bundle of sweet herbs, and a little pepper and salt; cover close, and let them stew half an hour. Give the pan a shake now and then. When they are just done, grate in a little nutmeg and a little beaten mace, and thicken it with a piece of butter rolled in flour; shake it all together for a few minutes; then take out the sweet herbs, lay the duck in a dish, and pour the sauce over it. Garnish with mint, chopped fine.

Potted Sea-Ducks.—Parboil the gizzards, livers, and hearts; chop them fine; mix with bread-crumbs and butter, seasoned with pepper and salt, and if you like, a little minced onion and sage. Fill the bodies and crops with the stuffing, and sew them up. Then have ready a pot with some boiling water in it, and a couple of sticks laid across, in the form of an X, so as not to touch the water. Lay the ducks on these; place them over the fire, and let them remain till quite tender, keeping the pot closely covered, so as to prevent the escape of the savor with the steam.

Next lay slices of parboiled pork on the bottom of a clean pot; lay the ducks in; cook, and turn, till of a fine brown. Make gravy as for other poultry, and serve with currrant jelly.

Roast Chickens.—Observe the previous directions as for roasting turkey; and if you wish to do several at once, put the spit through the bodies the other way. To roast chickens takes about an hour. If they are small they will do in three quarters of an hour.

Roast Chicken—another way.—Draw, singe, and truss the chicken, and put it between some slices of bacon; take care to tie up the legs on the spit, so that they be kept firm; baste it with its own gravy; when done to a point, (*i. e.* half an hour,) serve with cresses round it, seaoned with vinegar and salt.

Chicken Fricassee.—Half boil a chicken in a little water, let it cool, then cut it up, and simmer in a gravy made of some of the water in which it was boiled, and the neck, head, feet, liver, and gizzard stewed well together. Add an onion, a faggot of herbs, pepper and salt, and thicken with butter rolled in flour added to the strained liquor with a little nutmeg, then give it a boil, and add a pint of cream. stir over the fire, but do not let it boil. Put the hot chicken into a dish, pour the sauce over it, add some fried forcemeat balls, and garnish with slices of lemon.

Boiled Fowls.—Flour a white cloth, and put the fowls in cold water let them simmer three quarters of an hour, serve with parsley and butter, or oyster or celery sauce. The fowls may be covered with a white sauce if sent cold to table.

Boiled Fowls with Oysters.—Take a young fowl, fill the inside with oysters, put it into a jar and plunge the jar in a kettle or saucepan of water. Boil it for one hour and a half. There will be a quantity of gravy from the juices of the fowl and oysters in the jar; make it into a white sauce, with the addition of egg, cream, or a little flour and butter; add oysters to it, or serve it up plain with the fowl. The gravy that comes from a fowl dressed in this manner will be a stiff jelly the next day; the fowl will be very white and tender, and of an exceedingly fine flavor.

Chicken Pie.—Wash and cut the chicken (it should be young and tender,) in pieces, and put it in a dish; then season it to your taste with salt, pepper, a blade or two of mace, and some nutmeg. When your paste is ready for the chicken, put it in, and fill it about two-thirds with water; add several lumps of good sweet butter, and put on the top crust. A pie with one chicken will require from one hour to three-quarters of an hour to bake.

Fowl, Cold, to dress.—Take the remains of a cold fowl, remove the skin, then the bones, leaving the flesh in as large pieces as possible; dredge with flour, and fry a light brown in butter: toss it up in a good gravy well seasoned, thicken with butter rolled in flour, flavor with lemon, and serve hot with sippets.

Chicken Currie. Cut up the chicken raw, slice onions, and fry both in butter with great care, of a fine light brown; or, if you use chickens that have been dressed, fry only the onions. Lay the joints, cut into two or three pieces each, into a stew-pan, with a veal or mutton gravy, and a clove or two of garlick. Simmer till the chicken is quite tender. Half an hour before you serve it, rub smooth a spoonful or two of currie-powder, a spoonful of flour, and an ounce of butter; and add this, with four large spoonfuls of cream, to the stew. Salt to your taste. *When serving,* squeeze in a little lemon.

Fowl Broiled.—Separate the back of the fowl and lay the two sides open, skewer the wings as for roasting, season well with pepper and salt, and broil; send to table with the inside of the fowl to the surface of the dish; it is an admirable breakfast dish when a journey is to be performed.

Chicken Fricassee with Green Corn.—Cut the corn from the cob cover with water and stew until nearly done—cut up your chicken, put it in with the corn, and let them simmer for half an hour. Put in a little pepper and a tea cup of cream or milk, thicken with flour, stir in some butter—put your salt in ast.

To Roast Partridges.—Pick, draw, singe, and clean them the sam as fowls. Make a slit in the neck and draw out the craw; twist the neck round the wing and bring the head round to the side of the breast. The legs and wings are trussed the same as fowls, only the feet are left on and crossed over one another. Put them down to a clear fire and baste well with butter. When about half done, dust a little flour over them; let them be nicely browned. They will require to roast from twenty minutes to half an hour each. Serve on toasted bread dipped in the gravy, with gravy and bread-sauce.

To Roast Pigeons.—Pick, draw, and truss them, keeping on the feet. Chop the liver with some parsley, add crumbs of bread, pepper, salt, and a little butter; put this stuffing inside. Slit one of the legs, and slip the other through ii; skewer and roast them half an hour; baste them well with butter. Serve with brown gravy in a boat and bread-sauce

Pigeons in Jelly.—Make some jelly of calf's foot, or if you have the liquor in which a knuckle of veal has been boiled, it will answer the same purpose; place it in a stewpan with a bunch of sweet herbs, a blade of mace, white pepper, a slice of lean bacon, some lemon peel, and the pigeons, which, being trussed and their necks propped up to make them appear natural, season to your palate. Bake them; when they are done remove them from the liquor, but keep them covered close, that their color may be preserved. Remove the fat, boil the whites of a couple of eggs with the jelly to clear it, and strain it; this is usually done by dipping a cloth into boiling water, and straining it through it, as it prevents anything like scum or dirt sweeping through the strainer. Put the jelly rough over and round the pigeons.

To roast Snipes or Woodcocks.—These are not drawn. Spit them on a small bird-spit, flour and baste them with a piece of butter, lay a slice of bread toasted brown in the dish, and set it under the snipes for the trail to drop on. When they are done enough, take them up and lay them on a toast. Have ready, for two snipes, a quarter of a pint of good gravy and butter; pour it into a dish, and set it over a chafing-dish for a few minutes. Garnish with lemon.

To roast a Rabbit.—Having drawn and skinned it, wash it in warm water, dry it, truss it, and stuff it as follows—Beef-suet chopped fine; a few bread-crumbs; a little thyme, marjoram, and savory; a little grated lemon-peel, pepper and salt, mixed together with an egg; put it into the belly of the rabbit and sew it up. Suspend it before a good fire, and do not put it too close at first baste it well with but

ter or veal dripping, and dredge it two or three times with flour
When it is sufficiently roasted place the rabbit in a hot dish: put a
little water in a saucepan, a lump of butter rolled in flour, and pour
the gravy in from the dripping-pan; give it a boil up and pour it over
the rabbit.

To stew Rabbits.—Wash the rabbits well; cut them in pieces, and
put them in to scald for a few minutes. Melt a piece of butter in
which fry or brown the rabbits for a short time. When slightly
browned, dust in some flour; then add as much gravy or hot water as
will make sufficient soup. Put in onions, ketchup, pepper and salt, ac
cording to taste. Stew for an hour slowly.

GRAVIES.

GENERAL DIRECTIONS RESPECTING GRAVIES.—Gravy may be made
quite as good of the skirts of beef, and the kidney, as of any other
meat, prepared in the same way.

An ox kidney, or milt, makes good gravy, cut all to pieces, and pre
pared as other meat; and so will the shank end of mutton that has
been dressed, if much be not wanted.

The shank-bones of mutton are a great improvement to the richness
of gravy; but first soak them well, and scour them clean.

To dress Gravy that will keep a Week.—Cut clean beef thin, put
it into a frying-pan without any butter, and set it on a fire covered,
but take care it does not burn; let it stay till all the gravy that comes
out of the meat is dried up into it again; put as much water as will
cover the meat, and let that stew away. Then put to the meat a
small quantity of water, herbs, onions, spice, and a bit of lean ham;
simmer till it is rich, and keep it in a cool place. Do not take off the
fat till going to be used.

Clear Gravy.—Slice beef thin; broil a part of it over a very clear
fire, just enough to give color to the gravy, but not to dress it; put
that and the raw into a very nicely tinned stew-pan. with two onions.
a clove or two, whole black peppers, berries of allspice, and a bunch of
sweet herbs; cover it with hot water, give it one boil, and skim it well
two or three times; then cover it, and simmer till quite strong.

Cullis, or brown Gravy.—Lay over the bottom of a stew-pan as
much lean veal as will cover it an inch thick; then cover the veal
with slices of undressed gammon, two or three onions, two or three
bay leaves, some sweet herbs, two blades of mace, and three cloves

Cover the stew-pan, and set it over a slow fire; but when the juices come out, let the fire be a little quicker. When the meat is of a fine brown, fill the pan with good beef-broth, boil and skim it, then simmer an hour; and add a little water, mixed with as much flour as will make it properly thick : boil it half an hour, and strain it. This will keep a week.

Veal Gravy.—Make it as directed for cullis; but leave out the spice herbs and flour. It should be drawn very slowly; and if for white dishes, do not let the meat brown.

Gravy for Fowls without Meat.—Clean the feet and gizzard, and cut them and the neck into small pieces; put them into a saucepan with two small onions, a few sprigs of sweet herbs, a tea-spoonful of whole pepper, and some salt, and the liver, to which add a pint of water; simmer an hour; then mix the liver into paste with a little flour and butter; strain the gravy to it, stir well and boil up.

Strong Fish Gravy.—Skin two or three eels, or some flounders; gut and wash them very clean; cut them into small pieces, and put them into a saucepan. Cover them with water, and add a little crust of bread toasted brown, two blades of mace, some whole pepper, sweet herbs, a piece of lemon-peel, an anchovy or two, and a tea-spoonful of horse-radish. Cover close, and simmer; add a bit of butter and flour, and boil with the above.

SAUCES

Sauce.—Few things require more care than making sauces. As most of them should be stirred constantly, the whole attention should be directed to them; the better way is to prepare the sauces before cooking those articles which demand equal care; they may be kept hot in the bain-marie; butter and those sauces containing eggs ought never to boil. The thickest stew-pan should be used for making sauces and wooden spoons used for stirring them.

Melted Butter.—This must be made of fresh butter. Cut down the butter into small pieces, and put them into a small saucepan with cold water, in the proportion of an ounce of butter to a tablespoonful of water. Throw in flour for a dredger with the one hand, while with the other you turn the saucepan rapidly round, so as to cause the flour to mix without lumping. A small quantity of flour is sufficient. You now for the first time take the saucepan to the fire, and continue turning or shaking it till the butter is thoroughly melted. When it boils 't is ready; it should then have the consistency of rich cream. If it should oil in making, it may be partly recovered by putting a little cold water into it, and pouring it several times into and out of a basin

This sauce is the foundation of a number of other sauces, various additions being made to it for the sake of variety.

Oyster Sauce.—Save the liquor in opening the oyster, and boil it with the beards, a bit of mace, and lemon-peel. In the meantime throw the oysters into cold water, and drain it off. Strain the liquor and put it into a saucepan with them, and as much butter, mixed with a little milk, as will make sauce enough; but first rub a little flour with it. Set them over the fire, and stir all the time; and when the butter has boiled once or twice, take them off, and keep the saucepan near the fire, but not on it; for if done too much, the oysters will be hard. Squeeze a little lemon-juice and serve.

Lobster Sauce.—Pound the spawn, and two anchovies; pour on them two spoonfuls of gravy; strain all into some butter melted, as will be hereafter directed; then put in the meat of the lobster, give it one boil, and add a squeeze of lemon.

Another way.—Leave out the anchovies and gravy, and do it as above, either with or without a little salt and ketchup as you like. Many prefer the flavor of the lobster and salt only.

Sauce for Fowls of any sort.—Boil some veal-gravy, pepper, salt, the juice of a Seville orange and a lemon, and a quarter as much of port wine as of gravy: pour it into the dish, or a boat.

Onion Sauce.—Peel the onions, and boil them tender: squeeze the water from them, then chop them and add to them butter that has been melted rich and smooth, as will be hereafter directed, but with a little good milk instead of water; boil it up once, and serve it with boiled rabbits, partridges, scrag or knuckle of veal, or roast mutton. A turnip boiled with the onions makes them milder.

Mint Sauce.—Soak a bunch of young mint until all the gravel is removed from it, strip the stalks and chop up the leaves, then mix them with vinegar, water, and powdered white sugar. The sugar should be well melted before the sauce is served. It is generally eaten with roast lamb, and imparts to it a delicious flavor.

Bread Sauce.—Cut in slices the crumb of a French roll, to which add a few peppercorns, one whole onion, a little salt, and boiling milk enough to cover it, let it simmer gently by the side of the fire till the bread soaks up the milk, add a little thick cream, take out the onion, and rub the whole through a sieve, make it very hot, and serve with game or fowls.

Egg Sauce.—Boil three eggs hard, cut them in small squares, and mix them in good butter sauce, make it very hot, and squeeze in some lemon juice before you serve it.

Cod Sauce.—Take a bunch of parsley, chervil, two shalots, two cloves, a bay leaf, some mushrooms, a bit of butter, soak all together on the fire, adding a small spoonful of flour, and milk or cream sufficient to boil to the consistence of a sauce, and add to it some chopped parsley first scalded.

Eel Sauce.—Cut the eels into large pieces and put them into a stewpan with a few slices of bacon, ham, veal, two onions, with all sorts of roots, soak it till it catches, then add a glass of white wine and good broth, a little cullis, three or four tarragon leaves, chervil, a clove of garlic, two spices, and a bay leaf; simmer for an hour, skim it very well and sift it in a sieve for use.

Celery Sauce.—Three heads of fine white celery cut into two-inch lengths, keep them so, or shred them down as straws, boil them a few minutes, strain them off, return the celery into the stewpan, put either some brown or white stock and boil it until tender, if too much liquor reduce it by boiling; then add either white or brown sauce to it, season it with sugar, cayenne, pepper, and salt.

Superior Sauce for Plum Pudding.—Mix six yolks of eggs with four spoonfuls of sifted sugar and butter mixed together; have a pint of boiling cream which you will mix with your yolks, afterwards put it on the fire and stir it until it is of the consistency of sauce, then add to it a good wine-glass of brandy.

Tomato Sauce.—Fresh tomatos, take out stalk, press them all tightly down in a stewpan, cover them, put on the fire, strain off the liquor that is drawn from them, add to the tomatos a slice of raw ham, two onions, let it stew for an hour, then rub it through a sieve. Have in another stewpan a little good brown sauce, put your tomato into it, boil all together, season with cayenne, salt, sugar, and lemon juce.

French method.—Cut ten tomatoes into quarters and put them into a saucepan with four onions sliced, a little parsley, thyme, one clove, and a quarter of a pound of butter; set the saucepan on the fire, stirring occasionally, for three quarters of an hour; strain the sauce through a horse-hair sieve, and serve with the directed articles.

Apple Sauce.—Pare, core, and slice some apples, put them with a little water into the saucepan to prevent them from burning, add a little lemon peel; when sufficiently done take out the latter, bruise the apples, put in a bit of butter, and sweeten it.

Peach Sauce.—Take one quart of dried peaches, and wash them well soak them in enough cold water just to cover, until they are tender stew in the same water, until they are entirely dissolved. Sweeten with brown sugar, and send to table cold.

Cranberry Sauce.—This sauce is very simply made. A quart of cranberries are washed and stewed with sufficient water to cover them when they burst mix with them a pound of brown sugar and stir them well. Before you remove them from the fire, all the berries should have burst. When cold they will be jellied, and if thrown into a form while warm, will turn out whole.

VEGETABLES.

Observations on dressing Vegetables.

Vegetables should be carefully cleaned from insects and nicely washed. Boil them in plenty of water, and drain them the moment they are done enough. If overboiled they will lose their beauty and crispness. Bad cooks sometimes dress them with meat; which is wrong, except carrots with boiling beef.

To boil Vegetables green.—Be sure the water boils when you put the vegetables in. Make them boil very fast. Do not cover but watch them; and if the water has not slackened, you may be sure they are done when they begin to sink. Then take them out immediately, or the color will change.

Soft water is best for boiling vegetables; but if only hard can be obtained, a very small bit of soda, or carbonate of ammonia, will soften it.

To restore frost-bitten vegetables, lay them in cold water an hour before boiling, and put a piece of saltpetre in the saucepan when set on the fire.

Green vegetables, generally, will require from twenty minutes to half an hour, fast boiling; but their age, freshness, and the season in which they are grown, requires some variation of time. They should, almost invariably, be put on in boiling water.

POTATOES.

Potatoes require no attention for the preservation of their color, but their flavor will be spoiled if their dressing be not attended to, which, although of the most simple nature, is frequently ill performed. The best mode of doing it is to sort the potatoes, and choose them of an equal size; wash them with a scrubbing-brush, and put them into cold water sufficient to cover them and no more. About ten minutes after the water has come to a boil, take out the half of it, and replace it with cold. This, by attracting the heated vapor from the heart to the surface, dries the potatoes, and makes them mealy. When they are done

4*

pour off the water; remove the lid; sprinkle in a little fine salt; give the pot a shake and turn it down to the fire, so as to dry the potatoes, which the sprinkle of salt favors, by assisting in the escape of the steam. If you serve them mashed, let it be done quickly as possible.

Remove all specks; wipe out your kettle, put them back, and mash with a pestle, adding a piece of butter, or a cup of rich cream, or milk if you have it, with a little salt and pepper. After potatoes get ol l it is best to pare them, always, before boiling. You can, if you choose, brown your mashed potato in a stove oven; but it is very good without.

Potato Balls.—Mash boiled potatoes till they are quite smooth; add a little salt, then knead them with flour to the thickness required; toast on the griddle, pricking them with a fork to prevent their blistering. Eat them warm, with fresh butter; they will be found equal to crumpets, and much more nutritious.

Potatoes mashed with Onions.—Prepare some boiled onions by passing them through a sieve, and mix them with potatoes. Regulate the proportions according to taste.

Roasted Potatoes.—Clean thoroughly; nick a small piece out of the skin, and roast in the oven of the range; a little butter is sometimes rubbed over the skin to make them crisp.

Boiled Potatoes.—Rather more than parboil the potatoes; pare off the skin, flour them and lay them on a gridiron over a clear fire; send them to table with cold fresh butter.

Fried Potatoes.—Remove the peel from an uncooked potato. After it has been thoroughly washed, cut the potato into thin slices, and lay them in a pan with some fresh butter, fry gently a clear brown, lay them one upon the other in a small dish, and send to table as an *entre mets.*

To mash Potatoes.—Boil the potatoes as above; peel them, and remove all the eyes and lumps; beat them up with butter and salt in a wooden mortar until they are quite smooth; force them into a mould which has been previously floured, turn into a tureen which the flour will enable you to do; brown them before the fire, turning gently so as not to injure the shape, and when a nice color send to table. They are sometimes coated with white of egg, but they may be cooked without.

Potatoes fried whole.—When nearly boiled enough, put them into a stew-pan with a bit of butter or some good beef dripping; shake them about often to prevent burning, till they are brown and crisp; then drain them from the fat. It will be an improvement if they are floured and dipped in the yolk of an egg, and then rolled in finely-sifted bread crumbs.

Sweet Potatoes.—They should neither be pared nor cut; but select those that are neatest of a size, to cook together. When done, pour off the water and let them steam as other potatoes. They are sometimes half boiled, then cut in slices, and fried in sweet drip, ings, or butter The best way to keep them is to bury them in dry sand.

These are better roasted or baked than boiled.

To bake them.—Wash them clean and wipe them dry; then place them in a quick oven. They will take from a half of an hour to an hour, according to their siz.

To roast them.—Prepare them as for baking, and either cook them in the hot ashes of a wood fire, or in a dutch oven. They take from half to three-quarters of an hour to be done.

To boil Cabbages.—Cut off the stalk, and strip off the outer leaves, quarter, and wash them in plenty of water, and leave them to soak, top downwards, with a little salt in the water, for an hour or two. Put them into plenty of boiling water, with a good handful of salt and a bit of soda, and boil them till the stalk feels tender. Cabbages require boiling from twenty to forty minutes, according to their size. Drain them through a colander. Greens may be pressed between two plates.

To stew Cabbages.—Parboil in milk and water, and drain it; then shred it, put it into a stew-pan, with a small piece of butter, a small tea-cupful of cream, and seasoning and stew tender. Or, it may be stewed in white or brown gravy.

To pickle Red Cabbage.—Slice it into a colander, and sprinkle each layer with salt; let it drain two days, then put it into a jar, and pour boiling vinegar enough to cover, and put a few slices of red beet-root. Observe to choose the purple red cabbage. Those who like the flavor of spice will boil it with the vinegar. Cauliflower cut in branches, and thrown in after being salted, will look of a beatiful red.

To dress Cauliflowers:—Having picked them into small pieces, which is absolutely necessary in order to remove the slugs with which this vegetable abounds, wash it thoroughly in several waters, and let it lay to soak for full an hour before you dress it. Put it into a saucepan of boiling water, with a lump of salt, and when tender it will be done; let it drain in a colander, and serve it up with melted butter. Some persons may prefer to see them brought to table whole, but they must then take the chance of being helped, along with the cauliflower, to some unsightly insect, which would be sufficient to disgust the least delicate stomach; besides, if properly boiled, and laid carefully in the dish, the pretty appearance of the vegetable is by no means destroyed by its having been divided.

To boil Spinach.—Spinach requires more care in cleaning than any other vegetable. Each leaf must be picked separately from the stem or root, and washed in several waters. Put it in a colander to drain; after which put it into a saucepan to boil. If required to have a mild flavor, boil in a considerable quantity of water, but when the bitter of the spinach is liked, boil in very little water. It is usually dressed with hardly any water. Put in a little salt with it, and press it down frequently. Let it boil or stew till it is quite soft. When done, spread a towel over a colander, and pour the spinach into the towel. Then squeeze the water from it chop it fine, and put into a stew-pan with a little salt, and a bit of butter. After stirring and beating for a minute, put it into a flat dish, and make it in squares with a knife, cutting it quite through, for the sake of letting it be easily helped at table.

To boil Turnips.—Pare your turnips pretty thick, split them and boil them in plenty of water with salt in it for about half an hour, try them with a fork; if tender they are done; strain and serve them with a little melted butter in a boat, or mash them up with a little butter, pepper and salt. They should be boiled by themselves.

To boil Carrots.—Scrape and wash them, then split them in two, if very large into four, and cut them across; *Parsnips* are dressed in the same manner. When cold, they are very nice cut in slices and fried.

Asparagus.—Cut the heads about four or five inches long; scrape them and throw them into cold water; tie them in bundles; put them into boiling water with plenty of salt in it; let them come quickly to a boil—they will take from a quarter of an hour to twenty minutes. When tender take them up with a slice; drain them well; remove the string, and lay the asparagus in a dish, heads inwards, on slices of toast previously dipped in the liquor. Serve with melted butter. Sea kale is dressed in the same manner.

Beets.—They must not be scraped or cut, as they would then lose their color and sweetness. Salt the water, and boil them for an hour in summer, and in the winter for three hours. It makes a fine pickle if cut into slices when cold, and put into vinegar.

Onions.—Select the white kind, peel them, and put them into boiling milk, with a little salt, and let them boil from half an hour to three quarters. Drain them through a colander and serve them with melted butter.

Tomatoes baked.—Peel, and put them into a dish, with salt, pepper, and a little butter over them; then a layer of bread-crumbs, another of tomatoes; then more bread-crumbs, and so on until the dish be filled; the top is to be bread-crumbs. Bake three quarters of an hour or longer, according to the size of your dish. Some persons add nutmeg and sugar to the other seasoning.

To boil Beans.—After shelling, put them into boiling water with a handful of salt ; they will be cooked in about half an hour ; when the skins feel tender they are done enough ; strain them, and serve them with parsley and butter.

French or Scarlet Beans.—Cut off the two ends and string them, hen split and cut them in two, throw them into a pan of clean water, and put them into plenty of boiling water with salt and a little soda. When they are soft, which will be in about a quarter of an hour or twenty minutes, strain them through a sieve, and serve them with melted butter in a boat.

Green Peas.—A delicious vegetable, a grateful accessory to many dishes of a more substantial nature. Green peas should be sent to table *green*, no dish looks less tempting than peas if they wear an autumnal aspect. Peas should also be young, and as short a time as possible should be suffered to elapse between the periods of shelling and boiling. If it is a matter of consequence to send them to table in perfection, these rules must be strictly observed. They should be as near of a size as a discriminating eye can arrange them ; they should then be put in a colander, and some cold water suffered to run through them in order to wash them ; then having the water in which they are to be boiled slightly salted, and boiling rapidly, pour in the peas : keep the saucepan uncovered, and keep them boiling swiftly until tender ; they will take about twenty minutes, barely so long, unless older than they should be ; drain completely, pour them into the tureen in which they are to be served, and in the centre put a slice of butter, and when it has melted stir round the peas gently, adding pepper and salt ; serve as quickly and as hot as possible.

To Dress Mushrooms.—Cut off the lower part of the stem, peel, and put them into a saucepan, with just enough water to keep them from burning ; put in a little salt, and shake them occasionally. When tender, flavor them with butter, pepper, and salt ; add wine and spice if agreeable. Serve on buttered toast.

Egg Plant.—Cut the egg plant in slices half an inch thick, and let it lay for several hours in salted water, to remove the bitter taste. To fry it put the slices in the frying-pan with a small quantity of butter, and turn them when one side is done. Be sure that they are thoroughly cooked. Stuffed egg plant is sometimes preferred to fried. Peel the plant whole, cut it in two, and let it lay in salted water. Then scoop out the inside of the plant, chop it up fine, mixing crumbs of bread, salt and butter with it ; fry it, return it to the hollow egg plant —join the cut pieces together, and let them bake awhile in an oven.

Sweet Corn.—Corn is much sweeter to be boiled on the cob. If made into succotash, cut it from the cobs, and boil it with Lima beans, and a few slices of salt pork. It requires boiling from fifteen to thirty min utes, according to its age.

Dried Sweet Corn.—Put it in soak over night, in warm water enough to cover, and set it in a warm place. The next day put it to the fire in the same water, with more, if necessary, and keep it near the boil ing point for three hours ; but on no account let it boil, as this har dens the corn, and injures the sweetness. Be careful not to get too much water, for it is all to be retained ; and watch to see that it is not in danger of burning, keeping it wet with only just so much as it will finally absorb. Serve hot, seasoned with butter, pepper, and salt. Corn prepared in this way is almost as good as when fresh.

To Dry Sweet Corn.—Scald the ears in boiling water, until the milk is set, then take them up into a large tray, and get the corn off the cob, This is most expeditiously done, by passing the blade of an iron spoon slightly inclined to the cob, down the rows. Spread on large cloths ; and dry in the sun.

Succotash.—About two parts of beans, to one of corn [dried or green] makes the best succotash—prepare the corn same as above, stew the beans well, a piece of salt pork gives a nice flavor, mix well together, and season, with salt, pepper and butter.

Squashes.—Cut up the squashes in pieces of an inch thick, having first pared the squash ; if old, extract the seeds and boil the pieces until they break, mash them with a spoon, boil them a little longer and when they are done, squeeze them through a colander. Mix them with a little salt and a small quantity of butter.

Salad.—Take one or two lettuces, split them in two, thoroughly wash them, and drain the water from them, then cut them into small pieces, and then mix them with small salad, celery, and beet root; cut in small pieces some young radishes, cut into small pieces sliced cucumber, and an egg boiled hard cut into pieces and garnished about them. Make a sauce with the yolks of two eggs boiled hard, which rub well together in a basin with a wooden spoon, add a little pepper, salt, and mustard, when these are mixed to a smooth paste put in a few tea-spoonfuls of sweet oil, mixing it well between each spoonful ; then mix in a few tea-spoonfuls of vinegar in the same manner ; when the sauce is mixed according to the directions, it will never require shaking, and will always look like cream ; pour this sauce over the salad, or serve it in a cruet.

Coldslaw.—Shave as fine as possible a hard head of white cabbage, put it in a salad bowl, and pour over it the usual salad dressing.

Another way—is, to cut the cabbage head in two, shave it finely put it in a stewpan with half a tea-cupful of butter, a tea-spoonful of salt two table-spoonfuls of vinegar, and a salt-spoonful of pepper ; cover the stewpan, and set over a gentle fire for five minutes, shaking it occasionally. When thoroughly heated, serve it as a salad.

Cucumbers.—Let them be fresh as possible, or they will be unwholesome. Pare; cut off the stem end to the seeds, and slice in cold water, some time before they are wanted. Serve with salt, pepper, vinegar, and if you like, a little salad oil. Onions are sometimes sliced up with them—and tomatoes are frequently prepared in the above manner

---

EGGS, OMELETTES, &C.

It is very difficult to ascertain when eggs are perfectly fresh. There are different rules on the subject, but they are all liable to failure. One mode of judging, is to hold the egg between the eye and the light of a candle, shadowing the eye with the hand; if the appearance is universally luminous without any cloudiness, the egg is fresh; if cloudy or not uniformly luminous, it is probable that the egg is unfit for use.

To boil Eggs.—The boiling of eggs is a very simple operation, but is frequently ill performed. The following is the best mode:—Put the egg into a pan of hot water, just off the boil. When you put in the egg, lift the pan from the fire and hold it in your hand for an instant or two. This will allow the air to escape from the shell, and so the egg will not be cracked in boiling. Set the pan on the fire again, and boil for three minutes or more, if the egg be quite fresh, or two minutes and a half, if the egg has been kept any time. Eggs to be used hard for salads and other dishes, should be put into cold water, and boiled for a quarter of an hour after the water comes to the boil. In this case, the shells should not be taken off till the eggs are cold.

To Poach Eggs.—Take a shallow saucepan or fryingpan, and fill it about half full of water. Let the water be perfectly clean, not a particle of dust or dirt upon it. Put some salt into the water. Break each egg into a separate tea-cup, and slip it gently from the cup into the water. There is a knack in doing this, without causing the egg to spread or become ragged. A good way consists in allowing a little water to enter the cup and get below the egg, which sets the egg to a certain extent, before it is allowed to lie freely in the water. If the water be about boiling point, one minute is sufficient to dress the egg; but the eye is the best guide; the yolk must retain its liquid state.

lying in the centre of the white. Have buttered toasted bread prepared on a dish, and cut in pieces rather larger than the egg; then take up the eggs carefully with a small slice, pare off any ragged parts from the edges, and lay them on the bread. They may be laid on slices of fried bacon, when preferred.

Buttered Eggs.—Put a piece of butter in a saucepan, and melt it, adding a little milk. Break the eggs into a basin, and pour them into the saucepan. Season with salt and pepper, and continue stirring the eggs till they are sufficiently dressed. Serve on pieces of toasted bread.

Omelettes.—Omelettes are composed of eggs and any thing that the fancy may direct to flavor and enrich them. For a common omelette. take six eggs, and beat them well with a fork in a basin; add a little salt. Next take a little finely chopped parsley, finely chopped eschalot or onion, and two ounces of butter cut into small pieces, and mix all this with the egg. Set a fryingpan on the fire with a piece of butter in it; as soon as the butter is melted, pour in the omelette, and continue to stir it till it assume the appearance of a firm cake. When dressed on one side, turn it carefully, and dress it on the other. It will be dressed sufficiently when it is lightly browned. Serve it on a dish.

Omelette Fritters.—Make two or three thin omelettes, adding a little sweet basil to the usual ingredients, cut them into small pieces, and roll them into the shape of olives, when cold dip them into batter, or enclose them into puff paste, fry and serve them with fried parsley.

Onion Omelette.—Take two or three good sized onions, cut them into slices, and fry them in butter, when they are done add the yolks of two eggs, and a little chopped parsley, fry two small omelettes, on which lay the onions, with two or three anchovies cut in slices, roll them up lengthways, fry some pieces of crumb, cut the omelettes to the shape and size of these, and place them thereon, pour melted butter, and strew bread crumbs, and grated cheese over them, and color it in the oven. Omelettes may be judiciously varied by mincing tongue or ham with them.

BUTTER, CHEESE, ETC.

Butter—to Clarify.—Scrape off the outsides of the butter you may require and then put it into a stewpan by the side of a slow fire, where it must remain till the scum rises to the top and the milk settles at the bottom; carefully with a spoon take off the scum, when clear it is fi for use.

Butter preserved for Winter.—Take two parts of the best common salt, one part of good loaf sugar, and one part saltpetre, beat them well together; to sixteen ounces of butter thoroughly cleansed from the milk put one ounce of the above composition, work it well, and put it into pots when quite firm and cold.

Cheese toasted, or a Scotch Rabbit.—Toast a slice of bread, butter it, toast a slice of cheese on both sides, and serve it on the bread.

Cheese Fritters.—Take some mild brie or gruyere cheese, add some milk and butter, and put the whole into a saucepan, put to these ingredients flour, eggs, and sugar, make into a paste, of which form your fritters, fry them of a nice color and serve, then sprinkle with sugar, a small quantity of orange flowers may be added.

Welsh Rabbit—another way.—Toast a slice of bread quick on both sides and butter it, toast a slice of cheese on one side then lay that side upon your bread, then hold a hot salamander or shovel over the other side, spread it with mustard and a little pepper, keep it hot, and over it over.

PICKLES.

Rules to be observed with Pickles.

Keep them closely covered; and have a wooden spoon, with holes tied to each jar; all metals being improper. They should be well kept from the air; the large jars be seldom opened; and small ones, for the different pickles in use, should be kept for common supply, into which what is not eaten may be returned, and the top closely covered.

Acids dissolve the lead that is in the tinning of sauce-pans. When necessary to boil vinegar, do it in a stone jar on the hot hearth. Pickles should never be put into glazed jars, as salt and vinegar penetrates the glaze, which is poisonous.

Cucumbers.—Always select for pickling the small young and slender cucumbers, and leave about half an inch of the stem. This always makes cucumbers keep better. Put them into a strong brine as they are gath red. When you wish to green and prepare a portion of them for the table, cover the bottom and sides of your kettle with vine, or cabbage leaves; lay in the pickles; finish with a thick layer of leaves, and pour in cold fresh water enough to cover. Put the kettle over a moderate fire; bring it to the scalding heat; and keep them at that point until perfectly green. If in the course of ten or twelve hours they do not become so, renew the leaves, and repeat the process. When well greened, take them out; drain thoroughly; put them in a stone jar and pour over enough of the best cider vinegar, boiling hot, to cover them. This mode is adapted to any kind of pickle which is first put in brine, and then greened, to be put in vinegar.

To Pickle Tomatoes.—Throw them into cold vinegar as you gather them. When you have enough, take them out, tie some spices in a bag, and scald them in good vinegar. Pour the vinegar hot over the tomatoes.

To Pickle Red Cabbage.—Cut the cabbage across in very thin slices, lay it on a large dish, sprinkle a good handful of salt over it, and cover it with another dish; let it stand twenty-four hours, put it in a colander to drain, and then lay it in the jar. Take white-wine vinegar sufficient to cover it, a little mace, cloves, and allspice, and put them in whole, with one pennyworth of cochineal bruised fine, and some whole pepper. Boil it all up together, let it stand till cold, then pour it over the cabbage, and tie the jar over with leather.

Onions.—Boil some water with salt, pour it over the onions hot, let them stand all night, then peel and put them into cold salt and water. Boil double-distilled vinegar with white spice, and when cold, put your onions in a jar and pour the vinegar over them; tie them tight down with leather. Mind always to keep pickles tied down close, or they will spoil.

Peppers.—These are done in the same manner as cucumbers. If you do not like them very fiery, first extract the seeds. Peppers should never be put in the same jar with cucumbers; but tomatoes are much improved by being pickled with them. The bell pepper is the best for pickling. It should be gathered before it shows any signs of turning red. Peppers do not require any spice. They may be stuffed like mangoes.

Walnuts.—When they will bear a pin to go into them, place in a brine of salt and water boiled and strong enough to bear an egg on it, being quite cold first. It must be well skimmed while boiling. Let them soak six days, then change the brine; let them stand six more, then drain them and put them into a jar; pour over them a pickle of the best white wine-vinegar, with a good quantity of pepper, pimento, ginger, mace, cloves, mustard seeds and horseradish, all boiled together but co d. To every hundred of walnuts put six spoonfuls of mustard seed and two or three heads of shalot. Keep them six months.

To Pickle Mushrooms.—Take button mushrooms; rub and clean them with flannel and salt; throw some salt over them, and lay them in a stewpan with mace and pepper. While the liquor comes from them, keep shaking them well till the whole is dried into them again; then pour in as much vinegar as will cover them; warm them on the fire, and turn them into a jar.

Mushrooms prepared in this manner are excellent, and will keep for two years.

To Pickle Nasturtiums.—Pick them when young on a warm day; boil some vinegar with salt and spice, and when cold put in the nasturtiums; or they may be put into old vinegar from which green pickles or onions have been taken—only boil it up afresh.

To Pickle Beets.—Wash it, but do not cut off any of the rootlets; boil or bake it tender, peel it, or rub off the outside with a coarse cloth, cut it into slices, put them into a jar, with cold boiled vinegar, black pepper and ginger.

————

KETCHUP.

Tomato Ketchup.—Boil half a bushel of tomatoes until soft—force them throught a fine sieve, and put a quart of vinegar, one pint of salt, two ounces of cloves, two ounces of allspice, one and a half ounces of cayenne pepper, 1 table-spoonful of pepper, two heads of garlic skinned; mix together and boil three hours, then bottle with being strained.

Mushroom Ketchup.—Take a stewpan full of large-flap mushrooms that are not worm-eaten, the skins and fringe of those you have pickled, throw a handful of salt among them, and set them by a slow fire; they will produce a great deal of liquor, which you must strain; and put to it four ounces of shalots, two cloves of garlic, a good deal of pepper, ginger, mace, cloves, and a few bay-leaves—boil and skim very well. When cold, cork close. In two months boil it up again with a little fresh spice and a stick of horse-radish, and it will then keep the year, which mushroom ketchup rarely does, if not boiled a second time.

Walnut Ketchup (cheap).—Take walnut-skins and put them in a stone pan, let it stand covered up in a damp place for two or three weeks that the skins may decompose and ferment; the more decayed they become the better will be your ketchup. Then squeeze them through coarse cloths, and let the liquor drop into a clean pan; when you have pressed out all the liquor you can, pour a little water on the skins, and again squeeze them dry. Then put the liquor into a pot, with a good handful of salt, some allspice, and long pepper, and give it a good boiling for three or four hours, keeping it carefully skimmed. When cold, bottle it, and keep it in a dry, cool place. Should it afterwards turn mouldy or ferment, you need only boil it up and skim it, which will perfectly restore it. If it be properly made, many persons cannot distinguish it from the mushroom-ketchup, while the expense is comparatively nothing.

PIES AND PUDDINGS.

General Rules.—In boiling puddings, mind that the cloth be perfectly clean. Dip it in hot water and dredge it well with flour. If a bread-pudding, tie it loose; if a batter-pudding, tie it nearly close; apple and gooseberry pudding, &c., should be tied quite close. When you make a batter-pudding, first mix the flour well with milk, and stir in the other ingredients by degrees; you will then have it smooth without lumps. The best way, however, for a plain batter-budding is to strain it through a coarse hair-sieve, that it may have neither lumps nor the treadings of the eggs; and for all other puddings strain the eggs when they are beaten up. Be sure the water boils when you put your pudding in, and that it keeps boiling all the time, and that you keep it always covered with water; you should also move it about two or three times at first or it may stick to the pot; dip the pudding into cold water immediately you take it out, which prevents it sticking. If you boil your pudding in a dish or basin, butter the inside before putting the pudding in; the same should be done to the dish for a baked pudding or pie.

The quality of pie-crust depends much on the baking. If the oven be too hot, the paste, besides being burned, will fall; if too slack, it will be soddened, and consequently heavy.

Paste should be made on a cold smooth substance such as marble, with a light, cool hand. It should be made quickly; much handling makes it heavy. Great nicety is required in wetting the paste, too little moisture rendering it dry and crumbly, while too much makes it tough and heavy; and in either case, the paste cannot be easily worked. Practice alone can produce perfection in this art.

Before commencing to make paste for pies or puddings, it is necessary to place near at hand everything likely to be wanted, to inspect all the utensils, to prepare all the ingredients, and though last, not least to wash the hands and nails perfectly clean; for the hands are the best tools to make paste with.

Always use good sweet butter, dripping, or lard for pie or pudding crust. Some persons entertain the mistaken notion that butter which cannot be eaten on bread will do very well for paste, on the contrary the baking or boiling of rancid fat increases the bad flavor. It is a good plan to wash the butter in clean spring water before using it. Make two or three holes with a fork in the cover of your pies, that the steam may escape.

To Make Dripping Crust.—Take half a pound of fresh, clean dripping, and work it well up into a pound and a half of flour; rub it well in, and make it into a paste with water with the chill taken off. If worked well, it makes an excellent crust; some however, prefer butter, a quarter of a pound of which will be enough for a pound and a quarter of flour.

Puff paste for Fruit Pies or Tarts.—The paste for tarts is made much lighter than for meat pies. This is done by mixing a greater quantity of butter with the flour. The proportion of ingredients is half a pound of butter to two pounds of flour. Take one-third part of the butter which is to be used, and mix it with the flour, by rubbing together. If the butter is fresh, add a little salt. Put sufficient water to the flour to form it into a dough. Knead it quickly, and roll it out. Then divide the remainder of the butter into four or five equal portions. Spread one of these portions equally over the paste, by means of a knife. or sticking it over in small pieces. Dredge lightly with flour, and roll up the paste, with the butter inside. Flatten the paste again with the rolling-pin, and proceed in the same manner with the second portion of butter; then proceed with the third in the same manner, and so on, till all the butter is incorporated. In baking tarts, the oven should not be so hot as for meat pies.

Raised Crust for Meat-pies or Fowls, &c.—Boil water with a little fine lard, an equal quantity of dripping, or of butter, but not much of either. While hot, mix this with as much flour as you will want, making the paste as stiff as you can to be smooth, which you will make it by good kneading and beating it with the rolling-pin. When quite smooth, put a lump into a cloth, or under a pan, to soak till near cold.

Those who have not a good hand at raising crust may do thus: Roll the paste of a proper thickness, and cut out the top and bottom of the pie, then a long piece for the sides. Cement the bottom to the sides with egg, bringing the former rather farther out, and pinching both together; put egg between the edges of the paste, to make it adhere at the sides. Fill your pie, and put on the cover, and pinch it and the pie crust together. The same mode of uniting the paste is to be observed if the sides are pressed into a tin form. in which the paste must be baked, after it shall be filled and covered; but in the latter case, the tin should be buttered, and carefully taken off when done enough; and as the form usually makes the sides of a lighter colour than is proper, the paste should be put into the oven again for a quarter of an hour. With a feather, put egg over at first.

Rhubarb, Gooseberry, Plum, and Currant Pie.—Make a good crust; lay a little round the sides of the dish; throw some sugar on the bottom, and put in a little cup to suck in the juice; lay in the fruit, and put some more sugar at top; then put in a very little water; wet the top of the crust that goes round inside; put on the cover, and pinch the edges together. Cut the rhubarb into lengths of two inches, but do not skin it; only trim it at top and bottom.

Open Tarts.—Line your dishes with thin light paste, fill in with preserved fruits or jam, and lay strips of paste across in squares or diamonds. A short time will bake them.

Mince Pies.—Take equal weights of tender roast beef, suet, currants, raisins, and apples which have been previously pared and cored, with half their weight of soft sugar, one ounce of powdered cinnamon, an equal quantity of candied orange and lemon-peel, and citron, a little salt, and twelve sour almonds blanched and grated. Chop the meat and the suet separately; wash and pick the currants, stone the raisins and chop them with the peel; and having minced all the ingredients very fine, mix them together, adding a nutmeg.

Apple Pie.—Pare and take out the cores of the apples, cutting each apple into four or eight pieces, according to their size. Lay them neatly in a baking-dish seasoning with brown sugar, and any spice, such as pounded cloves and cinnamon, or grated lemon-peel. A little quince marmalade gives a fine flavor to the pie. Add a little water, and cover with puff paste, as above directed. Bake for an hour.

Rhubarb Pie.—Take the tender stalks of the rhubarb, strip off the skin, and cut the stalks into thin slices. Line deep plates with pie crust, then put in the rhubarb, with a thick layer of sugar to each layer of rhubarb—a little grated lemon-peel improves the pie. Cover the pies with a crust, press it down tight upon the edge of the plate, and prick the crust with a fork, so that the crust will not burst while baking, and let out the juices of the pie. Rhubarb pies should be baked about an hour, in a slow oven, it will not do to bake them quick. Some cooks stew the rhubarb before making it into pies, but it is not so good as when used without stewing.

Pumpkin Pie.—Halve the pumpkin, take out the seeds, rinse the pumpkin, and cut it into small strips, stew them over a moderate fire in just sufficient water to prevent their burning to the bottom of the pot. When stewed soft, turn off the water, and let the pumpkin steam over a slow fire, for fifteen or twenty minutes, taking care that it does not burn. Take it from the fire, and strain it when cool through a sieve. If you wish to have the pies very rich, put to a quart of the stewed pumpkin two quarts of milk, and twelve eggs. If you like them plain, put to a quart of the pumpkin one quart of milk, and three eggs. The thicker the pie is of the pumpkin the less will be the number of eggs required for them. One egg, with a table-spoonful of flour, will answer for a quart of the pumpkin, if very little milk is used. Sweeten the pumpkin with sugar, and very little molasses, the sugar and eggs should be beaten together. Ginger, grated lemon rind or nutmeg, is good spice for the pies. Pumpkin pies require a very hot oven.

Peach Pie.—Take mellow juicy peaches; wash and put them in a deep pie plate, lined with pie crust. Sprinkle a thick layer of sugar on each layer of peaches, put in about a tablespoonful of water, and sprinkle a little flour over the top; cover it with a thick crust, and bake the pie from fifty to sixty minutes.

Custard Pie.—Beat six eggs, sweeten a quart of rich milk, that has been boiled and cooled; a stick of cinnamon, or a bit of lemon-peel should be boiled in it. Sprinkle in a salt-spoonful of salt, add the eggs and a grated nutmeg stirring the whole together, line two plates with good paste, set them in the oven five minutes to harden; then pour in the custard and bake twenty or twenty-five minutes.

Cocoanut Pie.—Cut off the brown part of the cocoanut, grate the white part, and mix it with milk, and set it on the fire and let it boil slowly eight or ten minutes. To a pound of the grated cocoanut allow a quart of milk, eight eggs, four table-spoonsful of sifted white sugar, a glass of wine, a small cracker, pounded fine, two spoonsful of melted butter, and half a nutmeg. The eggs and sugar should be beaten together to a froth, then the wine stirred in. Put them into the milk and cocoanut, which should be first allowed to get quite cool; add the cracker and nutmeg, turn the whole into deep pie-plates, with a lining and rim of puff paste. Bake them as soon as turned into the plates.

Plum or Apricot Pie.—Take eighteen fine apricots, cut them in halves and take out the stones, place them in a dish lined with puff paste, add four ounces of powdered sugar, and four ounces of butter lukewarm, then put on the upper crust, glaze with the white of egg, and sprinkle sifted sugar all over, and bake in a moderate oven.

Open Tarts—These are tarts without covers, made in flat dishes. Cover the bottom of the dish with a common paste; then cut a strip of puff paste and lay round the edge of the dish. Fill in the centre with any jam or preserved fruit. Decorate the top of the jam with narrow bars of paste crossed all over, or stamped leaves. Bake for half an hour.

The above will answer for all kinds of Tarts.

Icing for Tarts.—After tarts are baked, they are sometimes iced on the top, to improve their appearance. The icing is done in the following manner:—Take the white of an egg, and beat it till it is froth. Spread some of this with a brush or feather on the top or cover of the tart, and then dredge white sifted sugar upon it. Return the tart to the oven for about ten minutes.

Plain Bread Pudding.—Weigh three quarters of a pound of any odd scraps of bread, either crust or crumb, cut them small and pour on them a pint and a half of boiling water to soak them well. Let it stand until the water is cool, then press it out, and mash the bread smooth with the back of a spoon. Add to it a teaspoonful of powdered ginger, moist sugar to sweeten, three quarters of a pound of picked and cleaned currants. Mix well, and lay in a pan well buttered ; flatten it down with a spoon, lay some pieces of butter on the top, and bake in a moderate oven. Serve hot.

Elegant Bread Pudding.—Take light white bread, and cut it in thin slices. Put into a pudding shape a layer of any sort of preserve, thin a slice of bread, and repeat until the mould is almost full. Pour over all a pint of warm milk, in which four well-beaten eggs have been mixed ; cover the mould with a piece of linen, place in a saucepan with a little boiling water, let it boil twenty minutes, and serve with pudding sauce.

Suet Pudding.—To a pound and a quarter of flour, add a pound of shred suet, with two eggs beaten separately, a little salt, and a little ground ginger, and just enough milk to make it ; boil it four hours. It is very nice the next day cut in slices and broiled.

Boiled or baked Custard Pudding.—Boil a pint of new milk ; let it stand until cold, and then mix it with four eggs well beaten, a little essence of lemon, and sufficient loaf sugar to sweeten it. If baked, a paste should be laid round the sides of the dish, and it will take twenty minutes in a moderate oven, if boiled, it will require ten minutes longer.

Lemon Pudding.—A quarter of a pound of suet, half a pound of bread-crumbs, four ounces of sugar, the juice of two lemons, the rind of them grated, and one egg. Boil it well and serve with pudding sauce.

Apple Pudding.—Four spoonfuls of apples boiled as for sauce squeeze into it the juice of two lemons, and the grated peel, add lump sugar, four eggs, a quarter of a pound of butter ; put all together in a thin crust. Bake it half an hour.

Plum Pudding.—Stone half a pound of raisins, wash clean and pick half a pound of currants. chop half a pound of beef or motton suet very fine, have some bread-crumbs made fine through a wire sieve cut fine a little candied orange, lemon, and citron, grate a little nut neg. a few grains of powdered cinnamon, break eight eggs ;[according to the size pudding required,] beat them up in a large basin, then add your spice and a quarter of a pound of fine sugar, then your candies, currants, and raisins, sweeten then a cup of cream or milk, add the grating of one lemon, mix in bread-crumbs till it is quite stiff and well mixed, add a glass of brandy and two of sherry, let it stand for some hours ; butter a plain round mould if you have it, sprinkle it all over with fried bread-crumbs. It will take three hours to steam. Pour sauce over it, any that may be approved. You will find it in another place in the book.

A plain Rice Pudding.—Well wash and pick eight ounces of rice, and put it into a deep dish, with two quarts of milk ; add to this two ounces of butter, four ounces of sugar, and a little cinnamon or nutmeg, ground ; mix them well together, and bake in a very slow oven. It will take about two hours.

Bread-and-Butter Pudding.—Grease a dish well with butter, then sprinkle in a good thick layer of currants, well washed and picked ; add some brown sugar, and cover with thin slices of light white bread until the dish is filled by alternate layers of currants, sugar and bread. Boil a pint of new milk, add four well-beaten yolks of eggs, a little nutmeg and grated lemon-peel ; pour into the dish containing the bread, &c., and let it stand for an hour, then bake in a moderate oven.

A paste may be put round the edge of the dish, but it is not necessary.

Apricot Pudding.—Split a dozen large apricots, remove the stones, and scald till quite soft. Pour a pint of boiling cream upon the grated crumbs of a penny loaf ; when nearly cold, add four ounces of sifted sugar, the yolks of four well-beaten eggs, and a wine-glassful of white wine. Pound the fruit in a mortar, with half of their kernels ; mix the fruit and the other ingredients together. Line your dish with paste, put a layer round the edge, pour in the mixture, and bake for half an hour.

Currant Pudding.—An excellent family pudding may be made of the following ingredients :—A pound of minced suet, a pound of bread crumbs or flour, three quarters of a pound of currants, washed and picked, a little powdered cinamon and grated nutmeg, and a very little salt. Beat two eggs, and add as much milk to them as will wet the whole. Mix all together, tie in a cloth as previously directed, and boil for three hours.

Batter Pudding.—Take a quart of milk, mix with six table-spoonfuls of flour, six well-beaten eggs, a table-spoonful of powdered ginger, and a tea-spoonful of salt ; flour a cloth that has been wet, or butter a basin and put the batter into it, tie tight, and plunge it into boiling water the bottom upwards. Boil for an hour and a quarter, and serve with plain melted butter, or sweet sauce. If according to taste, half a pound of well-washed currants may be added.

Indian Pudding, boiled.—Scald a quart of milk (skimmed n. lk will do), and stir in seven table-spoonful of sifted Indian meal, a tea-spoonful of salt, a tea-cupful of molasses or treacle, or coarse moist sugar, and a table-spoonful of powdered ginger or sifted cinnamon: bake three or four hours If whey is wanted, pour in a little cold milk after it is all mixed.

Potato Pudding.—Boil and mash some potatoes; mix with them some currants, sugar, and cinnamon, three or four eggs well beaten, some cream, enough to make it a thin mash; line your dish with puff paste, bake it brown in a brisk oven, not too much; strew white sugar over it when sent to table.

Apple Dumplings.—Pare a few good sized baking apples, and roll out some paste, divide it into as many pieces as you have apples, cut two rounds from each, and put an apple under each piece, and put the other over, join the edges, tie them in cloths, and boil them one hour.

Apple Dumplings, Baked.—Make them as directed above, but instead of tying them in cloths, place them in a buttered dish, and bake them

Suet Dumplings.—Make the paste the same as for suet pudding, wet your cloth, dust flour over it, put in the paste the size intended, tie up, and boil an hour.

Rice Dumplings.—Boil a pound of rice in two quarts of water till it becomes quite dry, then take it off, and spread it to cool, lightening the kernels with a fork. Pare a dozen juicy apples—scoop out the cores, and fill the cavities with lemon and sugar. Spread over every apple a thick coating of the boiled rice. Tie each in a separate cloth. Boil an hour and a half—be careful you do not break in turning them out.

Plain Indian Dumplings.—Indian dumplings are very good made plain, by merely wetting the meal with scalding water, or milk, and adding a little salt. You can, if you choose, boil the whole together in a mould or buttered bowl; cook at least four hours. If they are to be served for dessert, add a little molasses, and if you have it, a quarter of a pound of finely minced suet.

Damson Dumplings.—Line a basin with a good hot paste crust, roll it rather thin, fill it with damsons, cover it and boil it in a cloth for an hour; when done pour melted butter over it, grate sugar round the edge of the dish, and serve.

PANCAKES AND FRITTERS.

Rice Pancakes.—To half a pound of rice put two thirds of a pint of ater, boil it to a jelly ; when cold, add to it eight eggs, a pint of cream, little salt and nutmeg, and a half of a pound of butter melted ; mix weil, adding the butter last, and working it only so much as will make the batter sufficiently thick. Fry them in lard, but employ as little as it is possible to fry them with.

New England Pancakes.—Mix a pint of cream, five spoonfuls of fine flour, seven yolks, and four whites of eggs, and a very little salt ; fry them very thin in fresh butter, and between each strew sugar and cinnamon. Send up six or eight at once.

Fritters.—Make them of any of the batters directed for pancakes by dropping a small quantity into the pan ; or make the plainer sort and put pared apples sliced and cored into the batter, and fry some of it with each slice. Currants, or sliced lemon as thin as paper, make an agreeable change.—Any sort of sweetmeat or ripe fruit may be made into fritters.

Oyster Fritters—Blanch some of the largest oysters you can get but do not let them boil ; take off the beard, strain the liquor, and season with cayenne pepper and a few drops of essence of anchovies ; make this liquor into a good thick batter, using a little cream, have your stewpan with lard quite hot, then dip them separately into the batter, then fry them, use silver skewers for them, if not dish on a napkin and fried parsley.

Apple Fritters.—Take two or three large russeting apples, pare them, thin, cut them half an inch thick, lay them on a pie dish, pour brandy over them, let them lie two hours ; make a thick batter, using two eggs, have clean lard, and make it quite hot ; fry two at a time, a nice light brown, put them on the back of a sieve on paper, sift pounded sugar over them, glaze them with a shovel or salamander ; dish on a napkin.
After they are cut in slices take out the core with a small round cutter.

Potato Fritters.—Boil two large potatoes, scrape them fine ; beat four yolks and three whites of eggs, and add to the above one large spoonful of cream, another of sweet wine, a squeeze of lemon, and a little nutmeg. Beat this batter half an hour at least. It will be extremely light. Put a good quantity of fine lard in a stew-pan, and drop a spoonful of the batter at a time into it. Fry them ; and serve as a sauce, a glass of white wine, the juice of lemon, one desert-spoonful of peach-leaf or almond water, and some white sugar warmed together not to be served in the dish.

CUSTARDS.

GENERAL DIRECTIONS.

The common rule for these is eight eggs to a quart of milk; but you can make very good custard with six, or even four eggs to the quart. Custard may be boiled, or baked, either in cups, or one large dish. It may be put in a shallow paste, and prepared as a pie, or into a deep paste for a pudding. There should always be a little salt in the flavoring. The milk should always be boiled, and cooled again before being used; this makes it much richer.

Custards Boiled.—Boil one quart of sweet milk, with stick cinnamon. the rind of a lemon, and a few laurel leaves or bitter almonds, and sugar. Beat the yolks of eight eggs along with the whites of four of them ; add a little milk, and strain the egg into another dish. When the quart of milk boils, take it off the fire, and strain it ; then stir the egg into it. Return the whole to the saucepan, and set it on the fire again stirring constantly. Let it come to the boiling point; then take it off the fire, pour it into a large jug, and continue stirring it till it is nearly cold. It should now have the consistency of thick cream, and is ready for being poured into custard.

Rice Custard.—Boil one quart of milk, with a little salt, and any flavoring you like, and into this pour three table-spoonfuls of ground rice, mix smooth with a little cold milk, and one egg well beaten. Give it a boil up till it thickens, stirring constantly, and when cool put into cups.

Custard, Baked.—Boil a pint of cream with mace and cinnamon ; when cold, take four eggs, leaving out two of the whites, a little rose and orange-flower water, a little white wine, nutmeg, and sugar to your taste; mix them well together, and bake them in china cups.

Lemon Custard.—Take the yolks of ten eggs beaten, strain them, and whip them with a pint of cream ; boil the juice of two lemons sweetened with the rind of one, when cold strain it to the cream and eggs ; when it almost boils, put it into a dish, grate over the rind of a lemon, and brown it with a salamander.

CREAMS AND ICES.

Currant Cream.—Take some currants thoroughly ripe, bruise them in boiled cream, add beaten cinnamon, and sweeten to your taste ; then strain it through a fine sieve, and serve.

Strawberries and raspberries may be done in the same way. The fruit ought to be sweetened previous to putting in the cream, which should be used almost cold, else it is liable to curdle.

Ice Creams.—Split into pieces a vanilla bean, and boil it in a very little milk, till the flavor is well extracted ; then strain it. Mix two table-spoonfuls of arrow-root powder, or the same quantity of fine powdered starch, with just sufficient cold milk to make it a thin paste ; rubbing it till quite smooth. Boil together a pint of cream and a pint of rich milk ; and while boiling stir in the preparation of arrow-root, and the milk in which the vanilla has been boiled. When it has boiled hard, take it off, stir in a half a pound of powdered loaf-sugar, and let it come to a boil again. Then strain it, and put it into a freezer placed in a tub that has a hole in the bottom to let out the water ; and surround the freezer on all sides with ice broken finely, and mixed with coarse salt. Beat the cream hard for half an hour. Then let it rest, occasionally taking off the cover, and scraping down with a long spoon the cream that sticks to the sides. When it is well frozen, transfer it to a mould ; surround it with fresh salt and ice, and then freeze it over again. If you wish to flavor it with lemon instead of vanilla, take a large lump of sugar before you powder it, and rub it on the outside of a large lemon till the yellow is all rubbed off upon the sugar. Then, when the sugar is all powdered, mix with it the juice. Do the same for orange.

a lemon ; boil it up, then stir it till almost cold ; put the juice of a le-mon in a dish or bowl, and pour the cream upon it, stirring it till quite cold.

It is general eaten with preserves.

Orange Cream.—Pare four oranges very thin, into twelve spoonfuls of water, and squeeze the juice on six ounces of finely powdered sugar. Beat the yolks of nine eggs *well ;* add the peel and juice, beat them to-gether for some time. Then strain the whole through a flannel into a silver, or very nice block tin sauce-pan ; set it over a gentle fire, and stir it one way till pretty thick, and scalding hot, but not boiling, or it will curdle. Pour it into jelly glasses. A few lumps of sugar should be rubbed hard on the lemons before they are pared, or after, as the peel will be so thin as not to take all the essence, and the sugar will extract it, and give a better color and flavor.

Calves' Foot Jelly.—For one mould chop up two calves' feet, put them on in about four quarts of water to boil, this should be done the day before you require the jelly, keep it well skimmed and boil gently all day, it will then be reduced to about two quarts ; the next morning take off all the grease and wash the top with a little warm water, then rince it with cold, place the stock in the proper size stewpan to allow it to boil well, then put in a paring of lemon, without any white adher-ing to it, two or three cloves, a piece of cinnamon, a few bruised cori-ander seeds, and a bay leaf, let it boil for a few minutes then take it off to get cool. Have ready broken in a basin six or eight whites of eggs and the shells, chop them up together, squeeze five or six lemons, strain the juice, add sugar to the whites of eggs and a glass of cold wa-ter, then add the lemon juice ; add all this well mixed into the calves' foot stock, place it on your fire and let it rise to the top of your stew-pan, be careful it does not go over, then take it off the fire, place it on the cover and put some hot coals upon it, let it stand a few minutes. then run it repeatedly through the jelly bag until beautifully bright and clear ; flavor it with what may be required.

Rice Jelly.—Wash a large tea-cupful of rice in several waters. put it into a saucepan of cold water to cover it, and when it boils, add two cupfuls of rich milk, and boil it till it becomes dry ; put it into a shape and press it in well. When cold, turn it out and serve with pre-served currants, raspberries, or any sort of fruit round it.

Blanc Mange—Boil 1 ounce of isinglass, 3 ounces of sweet and 6 bitter almonds, well pounded in a quart of milk ; let it boil until the isinglass is disolved ; then sweeten it, stir it until nearly cold, and put it into the mould.

Rice Blanc Mange—Wash and pick a teacupful of rice, which boil in a pint of milk till quite soft. Sweeten or season it with pounded cinna-mon or grated nutmeg. Pour it into a shape, and, when cold, turn it out as already directed. It may be garnished with red or black cur-rant jelly, which is to be eaten along with it.

Marmalade.—Marmalade may be composed almost of any fruit, the best however for this purpose are apricots. peaches, oranges, quinces. eggs, plums, apples, &c., they are usually made by boiling the fruit and sugar together to a kind of pulp, stirring them constantly whilst on the fire; it is kept in pots which must not be covered till the marmalade is quite cold, the proportion of sugar is half a pound to each pound of fruit.

A Charlotte Russe.—Cut as many very thin slices of white bread as will cover the bottom and line the sides of a baking-dish, but first rub it thick with butter. Put apples, in thin slices, into the dish, in layers, till full, strewing sugar between, and bits of butter. In the meantime, soak as many slices of bread as will cover the whole, in warm milk, over which lay a plate, and a weight to keep the bread close on the apples. Bake slowly three hours. To a middling-sized dish use half a pound of butter in the whole.

JELLIES—PRESERVING, BREAD, &c.

PRESERVING.

General Directions.—Gather the fruit when it is dry. Do not boil the fruit too long, as that hardens it ; pour boiling water over the sieves used. Let the pots and jars containing fresh-made sweets remain uncovered for two days, then soak a split bladder and tie it tightly over the top; in drying it will shrink to the pot and render the latter perfectly air-tight. Keep preserves in a dry but not in a warm place. Be sure to use sufficient sugar ; this, with keeping them air-tight, is the only way to avoid the risk of their spoiling.

To Clarify Sugar for Sweetmeats.—For each pound of sugar allow half a pint of water, and for every three pounds, allow the white of an egg. Mix when cold, boil a few minutes, and skim it ; let it stand ten minutes, then skim it again, and strain it.

To Clarify Isinglass.—Dissolve an ounce of isinglass in a cupful of boiling water, skim it, and drain it through a coarse cloth. Jellies, candies, and blancmange should be made in a clean copper pot, or a bell-metal preserving-pan, and stirred up with a silver or wooden spoon.

Candied Fruits. – Preserve the fruit, then dip it in sugar boiled to candy thickness, afterwards dry it. Grapes may be thus dipped uncooked and then dried. Or fruit may be taken from the sirup when preserved rolled in powdered sugar, and afterwards set on a sieve to dry.

Red or Black Currant Jelly.—Strip the currants, put them in jars or pans, and bake them; strain off the juice through a sieve; having loaf sugar pounded and dried, in the proportion of one pound to one pint of juice set the juice over the fire, and when *boiling*, throw in the sugar gradu·ally, stirring the whole time; boil five minutes after all the sugar has been dissolved, if left too long over the fire, the jelly will become can-died. Pour into small-sized jars. By this method, the jelly will be perfectly clear without skimming, which saves waste and trouble.

Apple Jelly.—Take two dozen of large golden pippins or golden rus-sets; pare them and put in as much water as will cover them; let them boil as fast as possible till the apples are reduced to a pulp; strain them through a jelly bag, and to every pint of jelly put one pound of fine sugar; boil it over a quick fire for a quarter of an hour, add lemon juice to your taste, keep it boiling and skim it. Try a little on a plate; when it jellies, or sets, it is boiled enough.

Quince Jelly.—Pare, quarter, core, and weigh some ripe quinces, as quickly as possible, and throw them as they are done into part of the water in which they are to be boiled; allow 1 pint of this to each pound of the fruit, and simmer it gently until it is a little broken. Turn the whole into a jelly bag, or strain the liquid through a fine cloth and let it drain very closely from it. Weigh the juice, and boil for twenty minutes, take it from the fire and stir into it, until it is entire-ly dissolved, one pound of sugar for each pound of juice, keep it con-stantly stirred and thoroughly cleared from scum, boil from ten to twen-minutes longer, or until it jellies in falling from the skimmer.

Raspberry Jelly.—This is the most agreeable of all jellies. Crush the raspberries, and strain them through a wet cloth. Put the juice into a preserving-pan, with three-quarters of a pound of sugar to one pound of juice; boil it ten minutes, and take care that it does not darken, remove the pan off the fire; strain the juice through a bag and pour it into pots. Do not touch the bag till all the jelly has passed through, else it may become thick.

Rhubarb Jam.—Peel the stalks, and cut them up about an inch long; put them into a broad tin or copper pan with sufficient water to let them float. Let it boil till reduced to a pulp, keeping it well stir-red from the bottom. Pass the pulp through a colander or coarse sieve, and to each pint add from three-quarters of a pound to a pound of su-gar, either loaf or moist; put it back into the pan and boil it for anoth-er half hour, still keeping it stirred. Try now, by dropping a little on a plate, if it is done enough; it should be of the consistence of jelly; if it spreads, boil it a little longer, till stiff beneath the finger. Pour it into pots or jars, and when cold, cover and tie it down like other pre-serves

Cherry Jam.—Having stoned three pounds of cherries, bruise them and let the juice run from them; then boil together half a pound of red currant juice, and half a pound of loaf sugar; put the cherries into these whilst they are boiling, and strew on them three quarters of a pound of sifted sugar. Boil all together very fast for half an hour, and then put it into pots. When cold, put on brandy papers.

Blackberry Pie.—Allow three quarters of a pound of brown sugar to a pound of fruit. Boil the fruit half an hour; then add the sugar and boil all together for ten minutes.

Raspberry Jam.—Allow a pound of sugar to each pound of fruit, press them with a spoon in an earthen dish, add the sugar, and boil all together for fifteen minutes.

Gooseberry Jam.—To every pound of gooseberries add a pound of sugar; bruise the gooseberries in a mortar, and boil them well. When cold put the jam in pots.

Gooseberry Fool.—Pick a quart of full-grown unripe gooseberries, and put them into a saucepan with a little water. Cover them up and let them simmer very softly. When they are tender, but not so much done as to burst, take them off, strain the water from them, and turn them into a dish. Now bruise them to a fine pulp, and sweeten them with sugar to your taste. Let them stand till cool, and then add new milk or cream.

To Preserve Peaches, Apricots, Nectarines, and Plums.—Weigh the peaches, put them into a preserving pan full of cold water with a slice or two of lemon; set them on a slow fire, have ready a sieve and a napkin, and be careful not to do them too much.

Some of the peaches will be ready sooner than others; when they begin to be soft they are done enough; take them out as they become soft and drain them on a sieve, and let them stand until cold; then make a syrup, to every pound of peaches allowing a pound of loaf sugar; use some of the water in which the peaches were boiled for the syrup. Crack the pits of half a dozen peaches throw them into hot water and remove their skins, then boil them with the syrup you are making. Put the peaches into jars and glasses, and pour the syrup over them.

Cut several round pieces of paper, dip them in brandy, lay them over the preserves, and tie up the jars.

Apricots, Nectarines and Plums, may be preserved in the same manner.

This way of preserving peaches is much preferable to cutting them up and then preserving them. The fruit should not be permitted to boil until it becomes shrivelled.

5*

To preserve Green-gages.—Gather the finest you can get, and before they are quite ripe, put at the bottom of a bell-metal pot, some vine-leaves, roll your plums in vine-leaves, put alternate layers of plums and leaves till your pot is full ; cover them quite with water, put them over a very slow fire ; when the skin begins to rise, take them off and put them on a sieve to drain ; make a syrup with some of the faulty plums, put a pound of sugar to a pound of plums ; when the sugar is dissolved and skimmed quite clear, put in your plums and let them boil gently for ten or fifteen minutes ; take them off and let them stand in the pan till quite cold, then put them on again and let them boil very gently for twenty minutes or half an hour ; then take them out as free from the syrup as possible, and boil the syrup till it ropes, then pour it boiling over your plums. All kinds of plums may be done this way.

To preserve Strawberries and Raspberries whole.—To two pounds of fine large strawberries add two pounds of powdered sugar, and put them into a preserving kettle, over a slow fire, till the sugar is melted; then boil them precisely twenty minutes, as fast as possible ; have ready a number of small jars, and put the fruit in boiling hot. Cork and seal the jars immediately, and keep them through the summer in a cold dry cellar. The jars must be heated before the hot fruit is poured in otherwise they will break.

To preserve Quinces.—Pare, core, and halve the fruit. Boil the cores and parings, and strain the liquor. Boil the quince in the same until quite tender. Make a syrup with the liquor, allowing a pound of sugar to a pound of fruit. When the syrup is clear put in the quinces, a few at a time, removing them carefully as they are done, which will be in a few minutes. Boil the syrup until it is thick and clear.

Pine Apples.—Take pine-apples as ripe as you can possibly get them, pare them, and cut them into thin slices. Weigh them, and to each pound of pine-apple allow a pound of loaf-sugar. Place a layer of the pine-apple slices in the bottom of a large deep dish, and sprinkle it thickly with a layer of the sugar, which must first be powdered. Then put another layer of the pine-apple, and sugar it well ; and so on till the dish is full, finishing with a layer of sugar on the top. Cover the dish, and let it stand all night. In the morning remove the slices of pine-apple to a tureen. Pour the syrup into a preserving kettle, and skim it at least half an hour. Do not remove it from the fire, till the scum has entirely ceased to rise. Then pour the syrup, boiling hot, over the slices of pine-apple in the tureen. Cover it and let it stand till cold. Then transfer the sliced pine-apple and the syrup to wide-mouthed glass jars, or cover them well, pasting down thick white paper over the top.

To preserve Pumpkins.—Choose a thick yel'ow pumpkin which is sweet; pare, take out the seeds, and cut the thick part into any form you choose, round, square, egg-shaped, stars, wheels, &c.; weigh it; put it into a stone jar or deep dish, and place it in a pot of water to boil, till the pumpkin is so soft that you can pass a fork through it. The pot may be kept uncovered, and be sure that no water boils into the jar.

Take the weight of the pumpkin in good loaf sugar; clarify it, and boil the syrup with the juice of one lemon to every pound of sugar and the peel cut in little squares. When the pumpkin is soft, put it into the syrup, and simmer gently about an hour, or till the liquor is thick, and rich; then let it cool, and put it in glass jars well secured from air. It is a very rich sweetmeat.

Brandy Peaches, Plums, &c.—Gather peaches before they are quite ripe, prick them with a large needle, and rub off the down with a piece of flannel. Cut a quill and pass it carefully round the stone to loosen it. Put them into a large preserving pan, with cold water rather more than enough to cover them, and let the water become gradually scalding hot. If the water does more than simmer very gently, or if the fire be fierce, the fruit will be likely to crack. When they are tender, lift them carefully out, and fold them up in flannel or a soft tablecloth, in several folds. Have ready a quart, or more, as the peaches require, of the best white brandy, and dissolve ten ounces of powdered sugar in it. When the peaches are cool, put them into a glass jar, and pour the brandy and sugar over them. Cover with leather and a bladder. Apricots and Plums in the same way.

Preserving Fruit without Sugar.—It is a business that cannot so well be done in families as in large manufactories, where everything is arranged for convenience; but still with a little experience and careful attention, every family can save enough of the various fruits of the season to furnish their tables with a great delicacy during that portion of the year when they can get nothing of the kind. The whole secret consists in expelling the air from bottles or cans, by heat, and then sealing up the contents hermetically. If the article to be preserved is peaches, select such as you would for sweetmeats, and pair and cut them so they can be put in the bottle, and you must do this with the least possible delay, or they will be colored by the atmosphere. Some persons who want them to retain their natural whiteness, put them under water. When the bottle is full, cork it tight and wire down the cork with very little projection above the glass. When you have bottles enough to fill a kettle, such as may be most convenient, put them in and boil with the water all around up to the nozzle, for about fifteen or twenty minutes, or until the bottle appears to be full of steam, the atmosphere having been forced out through the cork. As soon as the bottles are cool enough to handle, dip the corks in sealing-wax so as to cover them quite tight. An additional precaution is used by some in putting tin foil over the wax.

Another plan is to cook the fruit slightly in a kettle, and then put it in cans or bottles, and pour hot syrup of sugar in to fill up the interstices, and then cork and seal. The heat of the fruit and syrup answering to expel the air. But the less they are cooked, or sweetened, the more natural will be the taste, like fresh fruit. when opened. We have eaten peaches a year old that we could not tell from those sugared an hour before.

Tomatoes are easily preserved, and retain their freshness better than almost any other fruit. The small kind are only used. Scald and peel them without breaking the flesh. Bottles should hold about a quart only, because when once opened, the contents must be used up at once. Bottles made on purpose, with large throats, and a ring on the inside are the best, and bottles are better than cans for all acid fruit. The cans, however, are more easily secured by solder, than the bottles by corks and wax, as the air is let out through a small puncture after the large opening is soldered up and cans heated, and that hole stopped with a single drop of solder.

Every article of fruit will keep fresh if the air is exhausted and the bottle sealed tight. The least particle of air admitted through any imperfection of the sealing will spoil the fruit. If the air could be driven out without heat, there would be no need of any cooking, and only just enough should be given to expel the air and not change the taste. Many persons prefer to add syrup made by about one pound of sugar to a quart of water, to all suitable fruits. Green corn, beans, peas, tomatoes, pie plant, currants, gooseberries, cherries, plums, raspberries, strawberries, peaches, are the most common things put up in this way. They add greatly to the pleasures of the table, and to the health of those who consume them; quite unlike, in that respect, the common preserves.

We have known fruit for pies put up in three-quart cans, by partially cooking in an open kettle in a syrup just sweet enough for use, and putting the fruit in the cans hot and soldering immediately. It kept thus perfectly.

Some fruits keep much better, and with less heating than others. Peas are among the hardest articles to keep; they contain so much fixed air.

We advise every family in the country to try this plan of putting up fruits for winter use, on a small scale this year, and if successful enlarge upon it next year.

Bread, Tea Cakes, &c.—In summer bread should be mixed with cold water. In damp weather the water should be tepid, and in cold weather quite warm. If the yeast is new, a small quantity will make the bread rise. In the country yeast cakes are found very convenient but they seldom make the bread as good as fresh lively yeast

Family Bread.—Take eight pounds of fine wheat flour, and sift it into your bread-dish ; rub well into the flour a table-spoonful of lard or butter. Make a deep hole in the middle of the flour, and having ready a quart of water, lukewarm, with a heaped table-spoonful of fine salt, mix it with flour and yeast, pour it into the cavity ; take a large spoon and stir in the surrounding flour until you have a thick batter ; then scatter a handful of flour over the dish, cover up your batter and put it in a warm place, if it is cold weather ; if summer anywhere will be warm enough. This is called *setting a sponge.* When the batter shows pretty determined signs of fermentation, pour in as much warm water as will make the whole mass of the flour and batter of a proper consistence. Knead it well, until it is perfectly clean and smooth ; put it directly into your bread-pans, which must be first well greased. In about half an hour it will be ready to put in the oven, which should be properly heated beforehand.

Large Bakings.—For large bakings, the following method is best. The common way is to put the flour into a trough, tub, or pan, sufficiently large to permit its swelling to three times the size it at present occupies. Make a deep hole in the middle of the flour. For half a bushel of flour take a pint of thick yeast, that is, yeast not frothy, mix it with about a pint of soft water, made blood-warm. The water must not be hot ; then gently mix with the yeast and water as much flour as will bring it to the consistence of a thick or soft batter, pour this mixture into the hole in the flour and cover it by sprinkling it with flour ; lay over it a flannel or sack, and in cold weather place it near—not too near, the fire. This is called *laying the sponge* ; when the sponge—or this mixture of water, yeast and flour, has risen enough to crack the dry flour by which it was covered, sprinkle over the top six ounces of salt, [more or less to suit the taste ;] mind, the time when the salt is applied is of great importance. We have seen directions in which we are told to mix the salt with the water and yeast. The effect of this would be to prevent fermentation, or, in other words, to prevent the sponge from rising. After the salt is sprinkled over the sponge, work it with the rest of the flour, and add from time to time, warm water [not hot] till the whole is sufficiently moistened ; that is, scarcely as moist as pie-crust. The degree of moistness, however, which the mixture ought to possess, can only be taught by experience ; when the water is mixed with the composition, then work it well by pushing your fists into it, then rolling it out with your hands, folding it up again, kneading it again with your fists till it is completely mixed, and formed into a stiff, tough smooth substance, which is called dough—great care must be taken that your dough be not too moist, on the one hand, and on the other, that every particle of flour be thoroughly incorporated. Form your dough into a lump like a large dumpling, again cover it up and keep it warm, to rise or ferment. After it has been rising about

twenty minutes, or half an hour, make the dough into loaves, first having shaken a little flour over the bread to prevent sticking. The loaves
may be made up in tin moulds, or if it be desired to make it into
loaves to be baked without the use of moulds, divide the dough into equal
parts, according to the size you wish to have your loaves, make each
part into the form of a dumpling and lay one dumpling, if we may so
speak, upon another—then, the oven being properly heated, by means
of an instrument called a peel—a sort of wooden shovel—put in your
loaves, and immediately shut the door as close as possible. A good
deal of nicety is required in properly placing the loaves in the oven—
they must be put pretty closely together. The bread will take from
an hour and a half to two hours to bake properly.

Brown or Dyspepsia Bread.—Take six quarts of wheat meal, rather
coarsely ground, one tea-cup of good yeast, and half a tea-cup of molasses, mix these with a pint of milk-warm water and a tea-spoonful
of saleratus. Make a hole in the flour and stir this mixture in the middle of the meal till it is like batter. Then proceed as with the fine
flour bread. Make the dough when sufficiently light into four loaves,
which will weigh two pounds per loaf when baked. It requires a hotter
oven than fine flour bread, and must bake about an hour and a half.

Rye and Indian Bread.—There are many different proportions of
mixing it—some put one-third Indian meal with two of rye ; others
like one-third rye and two of Indian ; others prefer it half and half.

If you use the largest proportion of rye meal, make your dough stiff,
so that it will mould into loaves ; when it is two-thirds Indian, it
should be softer, and baked in deep earthen or tin pans, after the following rule :

Take 2 quarts of sifted Indian meal ; put it into a glazed earthen pan,
sprinkle over it a table-spoonful of fine salt ; pour over it about a quart
of boiling water, stir and work it till every part of the meal is tho-
rougly wet ; Indian meal absorbs a greater quantity of water. When
it is about milk-warm, work in 1 quart of rye meal and a tea-cupful of
lively yeast, mixed with half a pint of warm water ; add more warm
water, if needed. Work the mixture well with your hands : it should
be stiff, but not firm as flour dough. Have ready a large, deep, well-
buttered pan ; put in the dough, and smooth the top by putting your
hand in warm water, and then patting down the loaf. Set this to rise
in a warm place in the winter ; in the summer it should not be put by
fire. When it begins to crack on the top, which will usually be
in about an hour or an hour and a half, put it into a well-heated
oven, and bake it nearly 3 hours. It is better to let it stand
in the oven all night, unless the weather is warm. Indian meal requires
to be well cooked. The loaf will weigh about 4 lbs. Pan bread keeps
best in large loaves.

Common Yeast.—Thicken two quarts of water with fine flour, about three spoonfuls; boil it half an hour. sweeten it with half a spoonful of brown sugar; when nearly cold put into it four spoonfuls of fresh yeast and pour it into a jug, shake it well together, and let it stand one day to ferment near the fire without being covered. There will be a thin liquor on the top, which must be poured off; shake the remainder and cork it up for use. Take always four spoonfuls of the old mixture to ferment the next quantity, keeping it always in succession. A half-peck loaf will require about a gill.

The bottles should be closely corked until the fermentation is over. After twenty-four hours the bottles may be well corked. They should be kept in a cold place. Yeast will not keep good over ten days unless it is made into little biscuits. For that purpose the process is the same as above, except that the yeast is taken from the bottles after it ferments, flour enough added to it to make a thick dough—it is then cut into biscuits and dried in the sun. Before the biscuits are used they should be soaked all night--the water from them is mixed with the bread. One biscuit to a large loaf or two small ones.

To Make French Bread and French Rolls.—Mix the yolks of twelve eggs and the whites of eight beaten and strained, a peck of fine flour and a quart of good yeast (but not bitter), with as much warm milk as will make the whole into a thin light dough; stir it well, but do not knead it. Put the dough into dishes, and set it to rise; then turn it into a quick oven; when done rasp the loaves.

French rolls are made by rubbing into every pound of flour an ounce of butter, one egg beaten, a little yeast, and sufficient milk to make a dough moderately stiff; beat it up, but do not knead it. Let it rise and bake in rolls on tins; when baked, rasp them.

To Make fine Rolls.—Warm a bit of butter in half a pint of milk, add to it two spoonfuls of small-beer yeast and some salt; with these ingredients mix two pounds of flour; let it rise an hour, and knead it well; form the rolls and bake them in a quick oven for twenty minutes.

Excellent Biscuits.—Take of flour 2 lbs., carbonate of ammonia 3 drachms in fine powder, white sugar 4 oz., arrow root 1 oz., butter 4 oz., 1 egg; mix into a stiff paste with new milk, and beat them well with a rolling-pin for half an hour; roll out thin, and cut them out with a docker, and bake in a quick oven for 15 minutes.

Tea Cakes.—Take of flour 1 lb., sugar 1 oz., butter 1 oz., muriatic acid 2 drachms, bi-carbonate of soda 2 drachms, milk 6 oz., water 6 oz. Rub the butter into the flour; dissolve the sugar and soda in the milk, and the acid in the water. First add the milk, &c. to the flour, and partially mix: then the water and acid, and mix well together, divide into three portions, and bake 25 minutes. Flat round tins or earthen pans are the best to bkae them in. If the above is made with baking powder, a tea-spoonful may be substituted for the acid and soda in the above receipt, and all the other directions carried out as stated above. If buttermilk is used, the acid, milk, and water, must be let out.

Milk Bread.—To 14 pounds of flour use a pint of yeast, 4 eggs, and milk of the warmth it comes from the cow; make it into a dough, the thikcness of hasty-pudding; leave it 2 hours to rise; sift over it a sufficient quantity of fine salt; work it with flour to a proper consistence. It takes a quick oven: always try a little bit before the bread is made up, as it will show the state of the bread as well as the oven.

A very light Potato Bread.—Dry 2 pounds of fine flour, and rub into it a pound of warm mealy potatoes; add warm milk and water, with a sufficient quantity of yeast and salt, at the proper time; leave it 2 hours to rise in a warm corner, in winter; bake it in tin shapes, otherwise it will spread as the dough will rise very light. It makes nice hot rolls for butter. An excellent tea or bun bread is made of it, by adding sugar, eggs, and currants.

Corn Meal Rusk.—Take 6 cups of corn meal, 4 cups wheat flour, 2 cups of molasses, 2 table-spoouful, of saleratus mix the whole together and knead into dough, then make two cakes of it and bake it three quarters of an hour.

Rusk.—1 cup of butter, 1 of sugar, 1 pound of flour, 1 pint of milk, 3 eggs, 1 cup of yeast, teaspoonful, bake in quick oven.

Corn Bread.—1 quart of milk, 4 eggs, tablespoon of sugar, 1 of butter, tea-spoonful of salt, some nutmeg, a large tea-spoonful of soda, and 2 of cream of tartar; stir in the meal until it makes a thick batter and bake in buttered tins in a quick oven.

India Johnny Cake.—1 quart, 1 cup of flour, 2 eggs, 1 cup of molasses 1 tea-spoonful of saleratus, 1 of ginger, then stir in the meal.

To Make Pancakes.—Beat up three eggs and a quart of milk; make it up into a batter with flour, a little salt, a spoonful of ground ginger and a little grated lemon-peel; let it be of a fine thickness and perfectly smooth. Clean your fryingpan thoroughly, and put into it a good lump of dripping or butter; when it is hot pour in a cupful of batter and let it run all over of an equal thickness; shake the pan frequently that the batter may not stick, and when you think it is done on one side, toss it over; if you cannot, turn it with a slice; and when both sides are of a nice light brown, lay it on a dish before the fire strew sugar over it, and so do the rest They should be eaten directly or they will become heavy.

Fruit Fritters.--Make a batter of flour, milk, and eggs, of whatever richness you desire; stir into it either raspberries, currants, or any other fruit. Fry in hot lard the same as pancakes.

Diet Bread.—One pound of flour, one of sugar, nine eggs, leaving out some of the whites, a little mace and rose water.

Wonders.--Two pounds of flour, three quarters of a pound of sugar half a pound of butter, nine eggs, a little mace and rose water.

A light cake to bake in cups.—One and a half pounds of sugar, half a pound of butter rubbed into two pounds of flour, one glass of wine, one of rose water, eight eggs, and half a nutmeg.

Sponge Cake.—Five eggs, half a pound of sugar, and a quarter of a pound of flour.

Another.—One pound of sugar, nine eggs, the weight of four eggs of flour; beat the yolks and white separate; mix the sugar and eggs together before you add the flour; a little nutmeg.

Another.—Five eggs, three tea cups of flour, two of sugar, and a little cinnamon.

Pound Cake.—Three eggs, nine spoonfuls of butter, three of sugar and three handsful of flour.

Bath Buns.—Take a pound of flour, the rinds of three lemons grated fine, half a pound of butter melted in a coffee-cup of cream, a tea-spoonful of yeast, and three eggs. Mix; add half a pound of finely powdered white sugar: work well, let it stand to rise well, and it will make thirty-nine buns.

Tea Cakes.—Take a pound of flour, half a pound of butter, and the same of sugar; the peel of a lemon finely grated, a little of the juice, an egg, a little brandy to flavor, and a tea-spoonful of bruised coriander seed. Roll it out thin, make into cakes, and bake them in a quick oven.

Short-Bread.—Rub one pound of butter, and twelve ounces of finely powdered loaf sugar, into two pounds of flour, with the hand; make it into a stiff paste with four eggs, roll out to double the thickness of a penny piece, cut it into round or square cakes, pinch the edges, stick slices of candied peel and some carraway comfits on the top, and bake them on iron plates in a warm oven.

Tea Cake.—One pound sugar, half pound butter, two tea-spoonful of pearlash, coffee cup of milk, mix stiff.

Composition Cake.—One pound of flour, one of sugar, half a pound of butter, seven eggs, half a pint of cream, and a gill of brandy.

Tea Cake.—Three cups of sugar, three eggs, one cup of butter, one cup of milk, a small lump of pearlash, and make it not quite as stiff as pound cake.

Loaf Cake.—Five pounds of flour, two of sugar, three quarters of a pound of lard, and the same quantity of butter, one pint of yeast, eight eggs, one quart of milk: roll the sugar in the flower; add the raisins and spice after the first rising.

Pint Cake.—One pint of dough, one tea-cup of sugar, one of butter, three eggs, one tea spoonful of pearlash, with raisins and spices.

Soft Gingerbread.—Six tea cups of flour, three of molasses, one of cream, one of butter, one table spoonful of ginger, and one of pearlash.

Wafers.—One pound of flour, quarter of a pound of butter, two eggs beat, one glass of wine, and a nutmeg.

Jumbles.—Three pounds of flour, two of sugar, one of butter, eight eggs, with a little carraway seed; add a little milk, if the eggs are not sufficient.

Soft cakes in little pans.—One and a half pound of butter rubbed into two pounds of flour, add one wine glass of wine, one of rose water, two of yeast, nutmeg, cinnamon and currants.

Rice Cakes.—Boil a cupful of rice until it become a jelly; while it is warm, mix a large lump of butter with it and a little salt. Add as much milk to a small tea-cupful of flour as will make a tolerable stiff batter—stir it until it is quite smooth, and then mix it with the rice.

Beat 6 eggs as light as possible, and add them to the rice.

These cakes are fried on a griddle as all other pancakes—they must be carefully turned.

Serve them with powdered sugar and nutmeg. They should be served as hot as possible, or they will become heavy—and a heavy pancake is a very poor affair.

Buck-wheat Cakes.—Take 1 quart of buck-wheat meal, a handful of Indian meal, and a tea-spoonful of salt; mix them with 2 large spoonsful of yeast and sufficient cold water to make a thick batter; beat it well; put it in a warm place to rise, which will take 3 or 4 hours or, if you mix it at night, let it stand where it is rather cool.

When it is light, bake it on a griddle or in a pan. The griddle must be well buttered, and the cakes are better to be small and thin.

Waffles.—Take a quart of flour, and wet it with a little sweet milk; then stir in enough milk to form a thick batter. Add a table-spoonful of melted butter, two eggs well-beaten, a tea-spoonful of salt, and yeast to raise it. When light, heat your waffle iron, by placing it on a bed of clear, bright coals; grease it well, and fill it with the batter. Two or three minutes will suffice to bake on one side · then turn the iron over; and when brown on both sides, the cake is done. Butter the waffles as soon as done, and serve with powdered white sugar and cinnamon; or you may put on the sugar and spice at the same time with the butter.

Muffins.—Take 1 pint of new milk, 1 pint of hot water, 4 lumps of sugar, 1 egg, half a pint of good brisk yeast, and flour enough to make the mixture quite as thick as pound-cake. Let it rise well; bake in hoops on a griddle.

Indian Griddle Cakes.—1 quart of milk, 6 eggs, tea-spoonful of saleratus, some nutmeg, tea-spoonful of salt, stir meal in until you have a thick batter, fry in melted butter and lard.

Dough Nuts.—4 and a half pounds of flour, 1 quart of milk, three-quarter lbs. of butter, same of sugar, one cup of yeast, a little salt and spice to taste, fry in hot lard.

Crullers.—2 lbs. flour, one half lb. of butter, 1 half lb. of sugar, 6 eggs and spice to taste cook same as dough nuts.

FRUIT CAKES, &c.

In making Cake, accuracy in proportioning the ingredients is indispensable. It is equally indispensable for the success of the cake that it should be placed in a heated oven as soon as prepared. It is useless to attempt to make light cake unless the eggs are perfectly fresh, and the butter good. Neither eggs nor butter and sugar should be beaten in tin, as its coldness prevents their becoming light. To ascertain if a large cake is perfectly done, a broad bladed knife shonld be plunged into the centre of it; if dry and clean when drawn out, the cake is baked. For a smaller cake, insert a straw or the wisp of a broom; if it comes out in the least moist the cake should be left in the oven.

Great attention should be paid to the different degrees of the heat of the oven for baking cakes: it should be, at first, of a sound heat, when, after it has been well cleaned out, such articles may be baked as require a hot oven; then, such as are directed to be baked in a moderately heated oven; and lastly, those in a slack or cooling oven. With a little care, the above degrees of heat may soon be known.

Frosting for Cake.—For the white of one egg, 9 heaping tea-spoons of white refined sugar, 1, Poland starch. Beat the eggs to a stiff froth so that you can turn the plate upside down without the eggs falling off, stir in the sugar slowly with a wooden spoon, 10 or 15 minutes constantly; to frost a common-sized cake 1 egg and a half.

Plum Cake or Wedding Cake.—One pound of dry flour, one pound of sweet butter, one pound of sugar, twelve eggs, two pounds of raisins, (the sultana raisins are the best,) two pounds of currants. As much spice as you please. A glass of wine, one of brandy, and a pound of citron. Mix the butter and sugar as for pound-cake. Sift the spice, and beat the eggs very light. Put in the fruit last, stirring it in gradually. It should be well floured. If necessary, add more flour after the fruit is in. Butter sheets of paper, and line the inside of one large pan, or two smaller ones. Lay in some slices of citron, then a layer of the mixture, then of the citron, and so on till the pan is full. This cake requires a tolerably hot and steady oven, and will need baking 4 or 5 hours, according to its thickness. It will be better to let it cool gradually in the oven. Ice it when thoroughly cold.

Brides Cake.—3 pounds of raisins, 2 of currants, 12 eggs, 1 pound of flour, 1 pound of sugar, 1 wine glass of brandy, 2 nutmegs, 1 table-spoonful of cinnamon, a half one of cloves, 1 of allspice, citron, mace, and bake in a quick oven, it will require 3 hours; this cake must be covered with icing.

Fruit Cake.—1 pound of flour, 1 of sugar, three-quarters of butter 2 of raisins, 2 of currants, 1 of citron, a half an ounce of mace, and a wine-glass of brandy, 1 of wine, 8 eggs, stir the sugar and butter to a cream, add the flour gradually, then the wine, brandy, and spice, add the fruit just before it is put in the pans; it takes over two hours if the loaves are thick.

Sponge Cake.—7 eggs, twelve ounces of sugar, six of flour, a little rose water, a spoonful of pearl ash.

Superior Sponge Cake.—Take the weight of ten eggs in powdered loaf sugar, beat it to a froth with the yolks of twelve eggs, put in the grated rind of a fresh lemon, leaving out the white part—add half the juice. Beat the whites of twelve eggs to a stiff froth, and mix them with the sugar and butter. Stir the whole without any cessation for fifteen minutes, then stir in gradually the weight of six eggs in sifted flour. As soon as the flour is well mixed in, turn the cakes into pans lined with buttered paper—bake it immediately in a quick, but not a furiously hot oven. It will bake in the course of twenty minutes. If it bakes too fast, cover it with thick paper.

Cream Cake.—Four cups of flour, three of sugar, one of butter, one of cream, five eggs, 1 table-spoonful of pearlash, mix the butter and sugar together first, then add the rest.

Queen Cake.—Mix 1 pound of dried flour, the same of sifted sugar and of washed currants. Wash 1 lb. of butter in rose-water, beat it well, then mix with it 8 eggs, yolks and whites beaten separately, and put in the drying ingredients by degrees; beat the whole an hour; butter little tins, tea-cups, or saucers, filling them only half full. Sift a little fine sugar over just as you put them into the oven.

Cocoanut Cakes —Take equal weights of grated cocoanut and powdered white sugar, [the brown part of the cocoanut should be cut off before grating it]—add the whites of eggs beaten to a stiff froth, in the proportion of half a dozen to a pound each of cocoanut and sugar. There should be just eggs enough to wet up the whole stiff. Drop the mixture on to buttered plates, several inches apart. Bake them immediately in a moderately warm oven.

Soft Ginger Cake.—One tea-cup of butter, one of milk, three of molasses, 4 eggs, 5 cups of flour, and one tea-spoon of pearlash. Make in to a stiff paste add bake in a slow oven.

A Plain Cake.—Mix together three-quarters of a pound of flour, the same of moist sugar, a quarter of a pound of butter, one egg well beaten and two table-spoonsful of milk; bake moderately.

Cookies—To three cups of sugar put one of butter, one of milk, three eggs, a tea-spoonful of saleratus dissolved in the milk, and carraway seeds, if you like, or other spice.

Cup Cake.—2 cups of sugar, 1 cup butter, 1 small cup milk, 3 eggs 4 cups flour, spice to taste.

Pint Cake—One pint of dough, one tea-cup of sugar, one of butter, three eggs, a tea-spoonful of pearlash, with raisins and spice to taste.

Macaroons.—Pound well in a mortar with the white of an egg half a pound of sweet almonds blanched, with a few bitter ones also blanched. Beat to a froth the whites of four eggs, and mix with them 2 lbs. of sugar. Mix all together, and drop them on paper placed on a tin. A half an hour in a gentle oven bakes them.

Tea Cake.—Three cups of sugar, three eggs, one cup of butter, one of milk, a small lump of pearlash; mix not quite as stiff as pound cake.

Loaf Cake.—Five pounds of flour, two of sugar, one and a half of butter, eight eggs, one quart of milk, roll the sugar with the flower, add yeast sufficient to make it rise, and then add the raisins and spice

Ginger Cake.—Two and a half pounds flour, 1 of butter, 1 of sugar, four eggs, one pint of molasses, tea-spoonful and a half of pearlash, one half pint of milk, two ounces of ginger, two pounds of currants, half a pound of raisins and a few cloves.

Buns.—Take one pound of flour, two ounces of butter, three of sugar, yeast to raise it, a little cinnamon or nutmeg, and milk enough to mould into biscuits. When light, bake to a fine, delicate brown.

Pounded Cake.—Mix a pound of sugar with three quarters of a pound of butter. When worked white, stir in the yolk of eight eggs, beaten to a froth, then the whites. Add a pound of sifted flour, and mace or nutmeg to the taste. If you wish to have your cake particularly nice, stir in, just before you put it into the pans, a quarter of a pound of citron, or almonds blanched, and powdered fine in rose-water.

Ginger Snaps.—Take two tea-cups of molasses, one of butter, and one of sugar. Boil the butter and sugar together. Add a table-spoonful of black pepper, two of ginger, a tea-spoonful of saleratus, and flour to roll out. Roll them thin; cut in shapes, and bake quick. These are very nice; and the longer they are kept the better they will be.

Sponge Ginger Bread.—Two pounds of flour, one of sugar, one of butter, six eggs, one pint of molasses, one pint of milk, two table-spoonfuls of ginger, one of cinnamon, one of cloves, two table-spoonfuls of pearlash.

Sponge Cake.—Ten ounces of flour, ten eggs, one pound of sugar.

Jumbles.—Stir together, till of a light color, a pound of sugar and half the weight of butter—then add eight eggs, beaten to a froth, essence of lemon, or rose-water, to the taste, and flour to make them sufficiently stiff to roll out. Roll them out in powdered sugar, about half an inch thick, cut it into strips about half an inch wide, and four inches long, join the ends together, so as to form rings, lay them on flat tins that have been buttered, and bake them in a quick oven.

Cheap Dough-Nuts.—Take two quarts of sifted flour, one cup of sugar, two tea-spoonfuls of cream of tartar, one of soda, one of salt, two cups of sweet milk, and flavor with cinnamon or nutmeg.

Plain Plum Cake.—Beat six ounces of butter to a cream, to which add six well-beaten eggs ; work in one pound of flour, and half a pound of sifted loaf sugar, half a pound of currants, and two ounces of candied peels ; mix well together, put it into a buttered tin, and bake it in a quick oven.

Seed Cake.—Mix quarter of peck of flour with half pound of sugar, quarter of an ounce of allspice, and a little ginger ; melt three-quarters of a pound of butter with half pint of milk ; when just warm, put to it quarter of a pint of yeast, and work up to a good dough. Let it stand before the fire a few minutes before it goes to the oven ; add seeds or currants ; bake one hour and a half.

Sugar Cake.—One pound and a half of sugar, one pound of butter, two cups of milk, two tea-spoonfuls of pearlash, three pounds of flour.

Another.—One cup of butter, half a cup of milk, one tea-spoonful of pearlash, seven eggs, six cups of flour, two cups sugar.

Composition Cake.—One cup of milk, one of butter, three of sugar, four of flour, and five eggs.

Washington Cake.—Beat six eggs very light, add one pound of butter, one of sugar, and one pint of rich milk a little sour, a glass of wine, a ground nutmeg, a spoonful of saleratus, bake in tins or small pans in a brisk oven.

Fruit Ginger Bread.—Four cups of flour, 1 of butter, 1 of sugar, 1 of molasses, one of milk, four eggs, three tea-spoonfuls of ginger 1 of cloves and nutmeg, half pound of currants, and raisins, add the fruit last, in an oven not very quick.

Queen Cake.—One pound of flour, one pound of sugar, one of butter, one wine glass of brandy, one nutmeg, add rose water, if you please, eight eggs.

Vanity Cake.—Three eggs, one cup of sugar, two tea-spoonfuls of cream of tartar, one tea-spoonful of saleratus, two of cream, one and a half cups of flour.

Drop Cake.—Mix half a pint of thick cream, half a pint of milk, three eggs, flour enough to render stiff enough to drop on buttered tins several inches apart—bake in a quick oven.

COFFEE, TEA, CHOCOLATE, AND COCOA.

Coffee and tea have now become such universal beverages for the morning or after dinner meal, that beyond a few general directions little remains for prefaratory matter.

Coffee should be purchased in the berry, and fresh roasted, it should always, when possible, be ground just previous to being made. After it is ground it should not be exposed to the air, as the aroma speedily flies off. If more is ground than required for the meal, keep it in a glass closely-stopped bottle. Coffee, like tea, should be an infusion not a decoction.

The best coffee is the Mocha, the next is the Java, and closely ap proximating is the Jamaica and Berbice.

Of tea little need be said; almost every one knows the rules for mak ing it.

Boiling water should alone be used.

Metal tea pots in preference to earthenware.

Silver is better than either.

A spoonful of tea for each person. Heat the tea-pot first with some boiling water, then pour that into the tea-cups to warm them; put in your tea, and pour enough water on to the tea to cover it; let it stand three or four minutes, then nearly fill the tea-pot with water, let it stand a few minutes, and pour out, leaving some portion of tea in the pot when you replenish, that all the strength may not be poured away in the first cup.

Chocolate can only be obtained pure of a first-rate house; that commonly sold is most infamously adulterated; the best Spanish or Italian chocolate should be purchased; the Florence has å high reputation.

Cocoa is the foundation of chocolate, it may be pounded, and either boiled as milk, or boiling water may be poured upon it. It is very digestible, and of a fattening nature.

Coffee, to Roast.—Coffee should never be roasted but when you are going to use it, and then it should be watched with the greatest care, and made of a gold color; mind and do not burn it, for a few grains burnt would communicate a bitter taste to the whole; it is the best way to roast it in a roaster over a charcoal fire, which turns with the hand, as by that means it will not be forgotten, which is very often the case when on a spit before the fire.

Coffee—to Make with Hot Water.—Instead of pouring cold water upon the coffee, boiling must be used, taking care the froth does not run over, which is to be prevented by pouring the water on the coffee by degrees.

Coffee—to Make with Cold Water.—Upon two ounces of coffee pour seven cups of cold water, then boil it until the coffee falls to the bot-

tom, when the froth has disappeared, and it is clear at the top lih
boiling water, it must be taken off the fire and be allowed to stan :
but as it often requires clearing a little cold water should be poured in
it the instant it is taken off the fire from boiling. A quicker way of
clearing it is by putting in a small piece of isinglass ; when it has stood
a sufficient time to settle, pour it off into another coffee-pot and it is
fit to use.

Coffee Milk.—Boil a dessert-spoonful of coffee in nearly a pint of milk
a quarter of an hour, then put in a little isinglass and clear it, and let
it boil a few minutes, and set it on the fire to grow fine.

Chocolate.—According as you intend to make this either with milk
or water, put a cup of one or the other of these liquids into a chocolate
pot, with one ounce of cake chocolate; some persons dissolve the
chocolate before they put it into milk ; as soon as the milk or water
begins to boil mill it; when the chocolate is dissolved and begins to
bubble take it off the fire, letting it stand near it for a quarter of an
hour, then mill it again to make it frothy ; afterwards serve it out in
cups.
The chocolate should not be milled unless it it prepared with cream ;
chocolate in cake should always be made use of in ices and dragees.

Cocoa.—To two ounces of good cocoa, allow one quart of water ; put
it in a covered saucepan; and when it comes to a boil remove it to a
place where it will just simmer for the space of an hour. Strain off; and
returning it to the saucepan, let it boil up, with the right proportion of
milk. Cocoa-shells may be prepared in the same way only that they
should be soaked several hours before being put to the fire. and boiled
two hours. Most people do not strain either cocoa, or shells.

Tea.—Tastes differ regarding the flavor of various sorts of tea: some
preferring all black ; others, all green ; and many, a mixture of both in
different quantities ; though most persons—when not fearful of their
nerves—agree that fine Hyson is the best. A good mixture, in point
of flavor, we know to be two fifths black—two fifths green, and one-fifth
gunpowder: all being, of course, superior quality.

Substitute for Cream in Coffee or Tea.—The white of an egg beaten
to a froth, mixed with a lump of butter big as a hazel-nut. Pour on
the coffee gradually, so it will not curdle ; and you can hardly distinguish the preparation from fresh cream.

INDEX.

WHAT TO SERVE AND HOW TO SERVE IT

Fulfilling a necessary need just after the ending of prohibition in the U.S.A. in 1934. Giving the basic information on wines and how to serve them. Explaining the various types and even what glasses to use. Ideal for finding out about the basic needs.

Pages 16 + 4 page colour Paperback

ISBN 0 946014 75 2   Price **$5**.00 including shipping

SWANK BY A YANK

First published around 1930 and written by an American for the British market, *"Being the inner mystery or the art of kidding"* includes such areas as an analysis of swank methods of swank the advertising swank. Making the most of what you have is as relevant today as when this book was first published.

Pages 96 Paperback ISBN 0 946014 72 8

Size 7¼"x5"   *Price* **$11**.00 including shipping

Available direct from PRYOR PUBLICATIONS
75 Dargate Road, Yorkletts, Whitstable, Kent CT5 3AE.
A full list of our publications sent on request.

DICK & FITZGERALD,

PUBLISHERS, NEW YORK.

Wilson's Book of Recitations and Dialogues. With Instructions in Elocution and Declamation. Containing a choice selection of Poetical and Prose Recitations and Original Colloquies. Designed as a Reading Book for Classes, and as an Assistant to Teachers and Students in preparing Exhibitions. By FLOYD B. WILSON, Professor of Elocution. This collection has been prepared with a special view to the development of the two cardinal principles of true Elocution—Voice and Action, and include a large proportion of Recitations and Dialogues, which appear for the first time in this form. The Colloquies are entirely original.
Paper covers. Price...**30 cts.**
Bound in boards, cloth back...**50 cts.**

Frost's Dialogues for Young Folks. A collection of Original Moral and Humorous Dialogues. Adapted to the use of School and Church Exhibitions, Family Gatherings, and Juvenile Celebrations on all Occasions. By S. A. FROST, author of "Frost's Original Letter Writer," etc. This collection of Dialogues is just what has long been wanted—it contains a variety that will suit every taste; some of the subjects are humorous, some satirical, hitting at the follies of vice and fashion, while others are pathetic, and all are entertaining. A few of the Dialogues are long enough to form a sort of little drama that will interest more advanced scholars, while short and easy ones abound for the use of quite young children. Most of the Dialogues introduce two or three characters only, but some require a greater number. The subjects chosen will, it is hoped, be found useful in conveying sound moral instruction as well as giving the opportunity to display memory and vivacity in rendering them.
Paper covers. Price...**30 cts.**
Bound in boards, cloth back, side in colors.........................**50 cts.**

The Parlor Stage. A Collection of Drawing-Room Proverbs, Charades and Tableaux Vivants. By Miss S. A. FROST. The authoress of this attractive volume has performed her task with skill, talent, and we might say, with genius; for the Acting Charades and Proverbs are really minor dramas of a high order of merit. There are twenty-four of them, and fourteen *Tableaux*, all of which are excellent. The characters are admirably drawn, well contrasted, and the plots and dialogues much better than those of many popular pieces performed at the public theatres. Any parlor with folding or sliding doors is suitable for their representation (or, if there are no sliding or folding doors, a temporary curtain will answer). The dresses are all those of modern society, and the scenery and properties can be easily provided from the resources of almost any family residence in town or country. The book is elegantly got up, and we commend it heartily to young gentlemen and ladies who wish to beguile the long winter evenings with a species of amusement at once interesting, instructive and amusing.
368 pages, small 8vo, cloth, gilt side and back, beveled edges. Price..**$1 50.**

Brudder Bones' Book of Stump Speeches and Burlesque

Orations. Also containing Humorous Lectures, Ethiopian Dialogues, Plantation Scenes, Negro Farces and Burlesques, Laughable Interludes and Comic Recitations, interspersed with Dutch, Irish, French and Yankee Stories. Compiled and edited by JOHN F. SCOTT. This book contains some of the best hits of the leading negro delineators of the present time, as well as mirth-provoking jokes and repartees of the most celebrated End-Men of the day, and specially designed for the introduction of fun in an evening's entertainment. Paper covers. Price....................................**30 cts.**
Bound in boards, illuminated..**50 cts.**

Frost's Original Letter-Writer. A complete collection of

Original Letters and Notes, upon every imaginable subject of Every-Day Life, with plain directions about everything connected with writing a letter. Containing Letters of Introduction, Letters on Business, Letters answering Advertisements, Letters of Recommendation, Applications for Employment, Letters of Congratulation, of Condolence, of Friendship and Relationship, Love Letters, Notes of Invitation, Notes Accompanying Gifts, Letters of Favor, of Advice, and Letters of Excuse, together with an appropriate answer to each. The whole embracing three hundred letters and notes. By S. A. FROST, author of "The Parlor Stage," "Dialogues for Young Folks," etc. To which is added a comprehensive Table of Synonyms alone worth double the price asked for the book. This work is not a rehash of English writers, but is entirely practical and original, and suited to the wants of the American public. We assure our readers that it is the best collection of letters ever published in this country. Bound in boards, cloth back, with illuminated sides. Price....................................**50 cts.**

Inquire Within *for Anything you Want to Know; or, Over*

3,700 *Facts for the People.* "Inquire Within" is one of the most valuable and extraordinary volumes ever presented to the American public, and embodies nearly 4,000 facts, in most of which any person will find instruction, aid and entertainment. It contains so many valuable recipes, that an enumeration of them requires *seventy-two columns of fine type for the index.* Illustrated. 436 large pages. Price....................................**$1 50**

The Sociable; *or, One Thousand and One Home Amusements.*

Containing Acting Proverbs, Dramatic Charades, Acting Charades, Tableaux Vivants, Parlor Games and Parlor Magic, and a choice collection of Puzzles, etc., illustrated with nearly 300 Engravings and Diagrams, the whole being a fund of never-ending entertainment. By the author of the "Magician's Own Book." Nearly 400 pages, 12 mo. cloth, gilt side stamp. Price..**$1 50**

Martine's Hand-Book of Etiquette and Guide to True Po-

liteness. A complete Manual for all those who desire to understand good breeding, the customs of good society, and to avoid incorrect and vulgar habits. Containing clear and comprehensive directions for correct manners, conversation, dress, introductions, rules for good behavior at Dinner Parties and the table, with hints on wine and carving at the table; together with Etiquette of the Ball and Assembly Room, Evening Parties, and the usages to be observed when visiting or receiving calls; deportment in the street and when travelling. To which is added the Etiquette of Courtship and Marriage. Bound in boards, with cloth back. Price..............**50 cts.**
Bound in cloth, gilt side.......................................**75 cts.**

Day's American Ready-Reckoner, containing Tables for

rapid calculations of Aggregate Values, Wages, Salaries, Board, Interest Money, &c., &c. Also, Tables of Timber, Plank, Board and Log Measurements, with full explanations how to measure them, either by the square foot (board measure), cubic foot (timber measure), &c. Bound in boards. Price...**50 cts**
Bound in cloth..**75 cts**

The Young Debater and Chairman's Assistant. Containing instructions how to form and conduct Societies, Clubs and other organized associations. Also, full Rules of Order for the government of their Business and Debates; together with complete directions How to Compose Resolutions, Reports and Petitions; and the best way to manage Public Meetings, Celebrations, Dinners and Pic-Nics. Also instructions in Elocution, with hints on Debate. This book is compiled from our larger work entitled "The Finger Post to Public Business." To any one who desires to become familiar with the duties of an Officer or Committee-man in a Society or Association, this work will be invaluable, as it contains minute instructions in everything that pertains to the routine of Society Business. 152 pages. Paper cover, price...30 cts.
Bound in boards, with cloth back, price.............................50 cts.

Frost's Laws and By-Laws of American Society. A condensed but thorough treatise on Etiquette and its usages in America. Containing plain and reliable directions for deportment on the following subjects: Letters of Introduction, Salutes and Salutations, Calls, Conversations, Invitations, Dinner Company, Balls, Morning and Evening Parties, Visiting, Street Etiquette, Riding and Driving, Travelling; Etiquette in Church, Etiquette for Places of Amusement; Servants, Hotel Etiquette; Etiquette in Weddings, Baptisms, and Funerals; Etiquette with Children, and at the Card-Table; Visiting Cards, Letter-Writing, the Lady's Toilet, the Gentleman's Toilet; besides one hundred unclassified laws applicable to all occasions. Paper cover, price...................................30 cts.
Bound in boards, with cloth back, price............................50 cts.

How to Cook Potatoes, Apples, Eggs and Fish, Four Hundred Different Ways. The matter embraced in this work consists of the combined contents of four little books which have obtained immense popularity in France and England, and which have been thoroughly revised and adapted for American housekeepers by an American cook of great experience. The work especially recommends itself to those who are often embarrassed for want of variety in dishes suitable for the breakfast table or, on occasions where the necessity arises for preparing a meal at short notice. Paper covers, price..30 cts.
Bound in boards, with cloth back, price............................50 cts.

Uncle Josh's Trunk-Full of Fun. A portfolio of first-class Wit and Humor, and never-ending source of Jollity, Containing the richest collection of Comical Stories, Cruel Sells, Side-splitting Jokes, Humorous Poetry, Quaint Parodies, Burlesque Sermons, New Conundrums and Mirth Provoking Speeches ever published. Interspersed with Curious Puzzles, Amusing Card Tricks, and Feats of Parlor Magic. Illustrated with nearly 200 Funny Engravings. This book consists of 64 large octavo pages, and contains three times as much reading matter and real fun as any other book of the same price. Illustrated cover, printed in colors, price...15 cts.

The American Housewife and Kitchen Directory. This valuable book embraces three hundred and seventy-eight receipts for cooking all sorts of American dishes in the most economical manner, and, besides these, it also contains a great variety of important secrets for washing, cleansing, scouring, and extracting grease, paints, stains and iron-mould from cloth, muslin and linen.
Bound in ornamental paper covers, price........................30 cts.
Bound in boards, with cloth back, price............................50 cts.

How to Cook and How to Carve. Giving plain and easily understood directions for preparing and cooking, with the greatest economy, every kind of dish, with complete instructions for serving the same. This book is just the thing for a young Housekeeper. It explains everything about the art of Cooking. It is worth a dozen of expensive French books. Paper covers, price...30 cts.
Bound in boards, with cloth back, price............................50 cts.

Spencer's Book of Comic Speeches and Humorous Recitations.

A collection of Comic Speeches and Dialogues, Humorous Prose and Poetical Recitations, Laughable Dramatic Scenes and Burlesques, and Eccentric Characteristic Soliloquies and Stories. Suitable for School Exhibitions and Evening Entertainments. Edited by ALBERT J. SPENCER. This is the best book of Comic Recitations that has ever been published, and commands a large sale on account of its real merit. It is crammed full of Comic Poetry, Laughable Lectures, Irish and Dutch Stories, Yankee Yarns, Negro Burlesques, Short Dramatic Scenes, Humorous Dialogues, and all kinds of Funny Speeches.

Paper covers. Price...**30 cts.**
Bound in boards, cloth back..**50 cts.**

Marache's Manual of Chess.

Containing a description of the Board and the Pieces, Chess Notation, Technical Terms with diagrams illustrating them, Relative Value of the Pieces, Laws of the Game, General Observations on the Pieces, Preliminary Games for Beginners, Fifty Openings of Games, giving all the latest discoveries of Modern Masters, with best games and copious notes. Twenty Endings of Games, showing easiest ways of effecting Checkmate. Thirty-six ingenious Diagram Problems, and Sixteen curious Chess Stratagems. To which is added a Treatise on the Games of Backgammon, Russian Backgammon and Dominoes, the whole being one of the best Books for Beginners ever published. By N. MARACHE, Chess Editor of "Wilkes' Spirit of the Times."

Bound in boards, cloth back. Price............................**50 cts.**
Cloth, gilt side..**75 cts.**

Martine's Sensible Letter Writer ;

Being a comprehensive and complete Guide and Assistant for those who desire to carry on Epistolary Correspondence ; Containing a large collection of model letters, on the simplest matters of life, adapted to all ages and conditions,

EMBRACING,

Business Letters ;
Applications for Employment, with Letters of Recommendation, and Answers to Advertisements ;
Letters between Parents and Children ;
Letters of Friendly Counsel and Remonstrance ;
Letters soliciting Advice, Assistance and Friendly Favors ;
Letters of Courtesy, Friendship and Affection ;
Letters of Condolence and Sympathy ;
A Choice Collection of Love Letters, for Every Situation in a Courtship ;
Notes of Ceremony, Familiar Invitations, etc., together with Notes of Acceptance and Regret.

The whole containing 300 Sensible Letters and Notes. This is an invaluable book for those persons who have not had sufficient practice to enable them to write letters without great effort. It contains such a variety of letters, that models may be found to suit every subject. Bound in boards, with illuminated cover and cloth back, 207 pages. Price............**50 cts.**
Bound in cloth ....**75 cts.**

The Perfect Gentleman.

A book of Etiquette and Eloquence. Containing Information and Instruction for those who desire to become brilliant or conspicuous in General Society, or at Parties, Dinners, or Popular Gatherings, etc. It gives directions how to use wine at table, with Rules for judging the quality thereof, Rules for Carving, and a complete Etiquette of the Dinner Table, including Dinner Speeches, Toasts and Sentiments, Wit and Conversation at Table, etc. It has also an American Code of Etiquette and Politeness for all occasions. Model Speeches, with Directions how to deliver them. Duties of the Chairman at Public Meetings. Forms of Preambles and Resolutions, etc. It is a handsomely bound and gilt volume of 335 pages.

Price..**$1 50**